JESUS IN JERUSALEM

Prelude to the cross

bert Bashford

DayOne

ENDORSEMENTS

It is a pleasure to commend this thorough and well-researched study of a neglected part of the last week of Jesus' ministry—from Palm Sunday up to Maundy Thursday. It helps us greatly by fitting all the Gospel accounts together, so that we see afresh something of the amazing authority and tenderness of our Saviour as he went to the cross for us. It will not only inform you, but move you to worship him anew.
Wallace Benn, former Bishop of Lewes

This is a careful, thorough and insightful study of each of the Gospel accounts of Jesus' life and teaching from the time of his arrival in Jerusalem on Palm Sunday until just prior to the evening of the Last Supper. This is not a book for quick perusal and will only reveal its riches to those who will give the time to work through each chapter in conjunction with reading the passages that are being discussed, which are all set out in the appendix. The author's aim is 'to engage the heart as well as the mind', and to this end each chapter, including the introduction, leads into a prayer that dwells on the aspect of the person and work of the Lord Jesus that has just been opened up.

Robert Bashford is a wise and experienced Bible teacher who has soaked his mind and heart in the texts, navigates some complex and rich material with great assurance, and invites us to dwell on the awesome nature of our Lord Jesus, the Living Word, the Messiah, the Judge, the Son of God, the Image of God, the Resurrection and the Life, the Teacher, the Son and Lord of David, the Guardian of the lowly, the Son of Man, the King and the Saviour of the World.
Rupert Bentley-Taylor, Bible teacher and retired pastor

Robert deftly and interestingly brings together the passages describing the Passion Week leading up to the Last Supper, and helpfully opens them up for us. Instructive, humbling, delightful and heart-warming. By God's grace it will do you a power of good. Warmly commended!
Ray Evans, Senior Pastor, Grace Community Church, Bedford, and the FIEC's Leadership Consultant

Robert Bashford gives us a careful and prayerful portrait of Jesus, in all his authority and tenderness, during the week leading up to his death on a cross. Follow along as he unpacks the exciting few days when the Messiah came to his capital city!
Lee Gatiss, Director of Church Society

Robert Bashford has served the wider church well by writing a thoughtful and reflective book on the final days of Jesus in Jerusalem. The shadow of the cross hangs over Jesus' various encounters that Robert so skilfully guides us through with fresh insights and understanding. He helpfully sets the scene and shows us the challenges that had to be faced by Jesus. You find here a careful use of the Scriptures as well as fresh light shed on some very familiar events. Anyone who is thinking about preaching on these great chapters from the four Gospels will find this book to be a great investment. I also like how each chapter ends with a lovely prayer that helps give the reader a focus once more on God and his gospel.

This little book could easily be the basis for church Bible studies during the season of Lent or Advent. Each chapter takes us a step nearer the cross. I found it particularly helpful, with the world in turmoil, to be reminded of the challenge that Jesus offers to all. Each chapter takes us quickly to the person and work of Jesus. The atmosphere of the time comes across strongly in every chapter. We also feel the struggles of Jesus as he walked willingly to his death. The book highlights the implications of the teaching he gave that still challenge us today.

Notwithstanding the research packed into this book, the writing is honest, clear and accessible. Here is a little book for everyone who is interested in the God-Man Jesus Christ. All will be blessed by spending time with Jesus in Jerusalem.
Peter Breckwoldt, Vicar, St John's Wimborne, and Member of General Synod

The clue to this book's aim and achievement lies in its subtitle: Prelude to the Cross. As an experienced Bible teacher and gospel preacher, Robert Bashford knows that to understand the final days of the Passion Week we need to grasp the sequence of events which preceded them.

For each section, Robert engages in detailed, systematic, theologically sensitive exposition of the parallel accounts while asking probing questions about the distinctive contribution of each Gospel writer. The reader is referred to the appendix, where parallel texts are helpfully laid out, encouraging readers to engage with the texts themselves and to follow the argument being advanced. Robert has clearly engaged with the vast literature on the Gospels, especially at points where there is a need to understand apparent discrepancies and contradictions.

Robert's stated aim 'to engage the heart as well as the mind' is fulfilled throughout the book, but is brought to a focus in the prayer with which each chapter ends, applying these truths as a preacher would. So *Jesus in Jerusalem* becomes not only a closely argued textual study but also a challenging sermon. 'He who has ears, let him hear'!
Martyn Hallett, former Pastor, Hope Church Goldington, Bedford

For my wife, Barbara

© Day One Publications 2020

ISBN 978-1-84625-674-5

British Library Cataloguing in Publication Data available

Published by Day One Publications
Ryelands Road, Leominster, HR6 8NZ
Telephone 01568 613 740 FAX 01568 611 473
email—sales@dayone.co.uk
web site—www.dayone.co.uk

Cover design by Kathryn Chedgzoy
Printed by 4edge

INTRODUCTION   9

1 THE COMING OF THE KING
(MATTHEW 21:1–11; MARK 11:1–11;
LUKE 19:28–44; JOHN 12:12–19)   22

2 THE FIG TREE AND THE TEMPLE
(MATTHEW 21:12–22;
MARK 11:12–25; LUKE 19:45–48)   28

3 CHALLENGE 1: A QUESTION OF AUTHORITY
(MATTHEW 21:23–22:14; MARK 11:27–12:12;
LUKE 20:1–18)   37

4 CHALLENGE 2: A QUESTION OF ALLEGIANCE
(MATTHEW 22:15–22; MARK 12:13–17;
LUKE 20:19–26)   47

5 CHALLENGE 3: A QUESTION OF LIFE AND DEATH
(MATTHEW 22:23–33; MARK 12:18–27;
LUKE 20:27–40)   51

6 CHALLENGE 4: A QUESTION OF IMPORTANCE
(MATTHEW 22:34–40; MARK 12:28–34)   54

7 CHALLENGE 5: JESUS ASKS A QUESTION
(MATTHEW 22:41–46; MARK 12:35–37;
LUKE 20:41–44)   58

8 JUDGMENT ON HYPOCRITES
(MATTHEW 23:1–39; MARK 12:38–40;
LUKE 20:45–47)   60

9 AN EXAMPLE TO FOLLOW
(MARK 12:41–44; LUKE 21:1–4)   70

10 BE PREPARED!
(MATTHEW 24:1–51; MARK 13:1–37;
LUKE 21:5–38)   72

11 **THE COMING KINGDOM**
    (MATTHEW 25:1–46)   88

12 **THE SAVIOUR OF THE WORLD**
    (JOHN 12:20–50)   96

APPENDIX: THE TEXTS OF THE FOUR GOSPELS
    FROM PALM SUNDAY TO JUST BEFORE
    MAUNDY THURSDAY EVENING   109

The focus of this study

The subject matter of this study concerns the record, in all four Gospels, of the first part of the final week of Jesus' ministry in Jerusalem, beginning with the Triumphal Entry. The accounts of the three Synoptic Gospels (Matthew, Mark and Luke) run along generally parallel lines but with some interesting variations in detail. Each contains material not found in the others. John's account similarly begins with the Triumphal Entry, but from there on John's material is independent of that of the other Gospel writers.

The present study finishes immediately before the Passion narrative of Maundy Thursday evening onwards. In each of the Synoptic Gospels (Matthew, Mark and Luke), that point is marked by the reference to the plot of the chief priests and scribes to have Jesus put to death and the decision of Judas Iscariot to betray Jesus (Matt. 26:1ff.; Mark 14:1ff.; Luke 22:1ff). In John's Gospel the Passion narrative begins at the start of chapter 13, where John turns his attention to the Upper Room on the Thursday evening.

So, to be specific about the Bible chapters and verses that cover the period of Jesus' ministry which we are focusing on, they are:

- Matthew 21:1–25:46;
- Mark 11:1–13:37;
- Luke 19:28–21:38;
- John 12:12–50.

These sections of the Gospels are set out in the Appendix in parallel columns, in order to facilitate comparison, except where only one of the Gospels includes material at a particular point, in which case the text of that material is spread over more than one column. In the Appendix the editorial headings from the ESV Bible are mostly followed. The changes that have been introduced are either in order to reflect the discussion in this book or in order to provide consistency of editorial headings for parallel passages. Paragraph divisions in the ESV text are retained, except for a very few changes, which again have been introduced in order to reflect the content of this book. All such changes are marked in the Appendix.

The aim of this study is to engage the heart as well as the mind. Each chapter, including this Introduction, ends with a prayer that flows out of the preceding discussion.

I have been drawn to these chapters of the Gospels, which are not studied as much as they deserve, because they include a wealth of material about the Person and the Work of the Lord Jesus Christ and about living as his followers in the light of eternity. It might be asked why this study does not continue into the events of Maundy Thursday, Good Friday and Easter Day. The answer is that a far larger work would be called for to do justice to that task, and many good books on that momentous weekend are already available.

The King comes to his capital

The dominant tone of Jesus' ministry in Jerusalem during this period of time is one of *authority* and *tenderness*—a remarkable combination of characteristics.

His *authority* is that of the King who has come to his capital. In his Triumphal Entry, Jesus lifts the cloak of secrecy on his identity and makes a public declaration that he is none other than the Christ (or Messiah) anticipated by Old Testament prophecy. He acts with authority in his cleansing of the temple. The cursing of the fig tree enables us to understand Jesus' action in the temple as a judgment, which he alone has the right to carry out. Jesus' authority is demonstrated in the series of debates with the city's religious leaders. They seek to silence him, by forcing him either to lose face before the crowds or to say something for which they can have him arrested. But each time Jesus turns the tables on his critics, exposing their duplicity and their inability to answer his challenges to them. Jesus is outspoken in his denunciation of the scribes and Pharisees, particularly exposing their hypocrisy. And Jesus spells out both the certainty of judgment to fall on the nation at the hands of the Romans within a generation, and the certainty of judgment on the world at his Second Coming.

Alongside Jesus' authority there is also *compassion and tenderness*. He heals the blind and lame in the temple. He defends the right of children to shout his praises. He weeps over a city—and a nation—which rejects him. He speaks encouragingly to a Pharisee who is 'not far from the kingdom of God'. He commends a poor widow, unnoticed by the crowds, for the extravagance of her giving. In addition, he announces publicly his role as the one who has come into the world to be its Rescuer.

A chronology for this period of time—four days?
The least important task in approaching this study is to work out a timetable for the few days under review. However, enough clues are to be found within the Gospel accounts to enable us to tie some events to particular days. It makes sense, therefore, to follow the evidence provided for us as far as it leads. Beyond that, we are in the realm of guesswork.

A case can be made for the recorded events taking place over a period of four days.

We begin with what we can be sure of.

The starting point is, of course, Jesus' Triumphal Entry into Jerusalem. It is not just a matter of tradition that this event took place on a *Sunday*. The day has come to be known as Palm Sunday. While Matthew, Mark and Luke give no specific indication regarding on which day of the week Jesus arrived in the capital, the information that John provides is precise. In John 12:1 he tells us: 'Six days before the Passover, Jesus therefore came to Bethany.' He goes on to record the dinner at which Mary, the sister of Martha and Lazarus, anointed Jesus with expensive ointment— an action which Jesus linked with his approaching death.[1] It makes best sense to understand the Passover as being on the Friday, but beginning on the Thursday evening (in accordance with the normal Jewish way of reckoning days). So 'six days before the Passover' would mean the Saturday of the previous week, but beginning on the Friday evening. The most natural understanding is that Jesus arrived at Bethany on the Friday evening, as Sabbath began, and that the dinner took place on the Sabbath, the Saturday evening. Therefore, when John tells us in John 12:12 that it was 'the next day' when Jesus entered Jerusalem, that day can be established as the Sunday.

So a case has been made for the traditional dating of the Triumphal Entry as the Sunday of that significant week. It is Mark who helps us to establish the general course of events over the following two days. With regard to the Sunday, he tells us that Jesus entered Jerusalem and went into the temple, where he looked around at everything. Then, he says, 'as it was already late, he went out to Bethany with the twelve' (Mark 11:11). It seems likely that Jesus stayed overnight during these few days with his friends Martha, Mary and Lazarus.

Monday, in Mark's Gospel, stretches from Mark 11:12, with its reference to 'on the following day', to Mark 11:19, where we are told, 'And when evening came they went out of the city.' This means that both the cursing of the fig tree and the cleansing of the temple took place on the Monday. Without this information from Mark, we might well have imagined that Jesus cleansed the temple the previous day, immediately following his arrival in Jerusalem. Matthew alone tells us about the healings in the temple at the end of the day (Matt. 21:14–16).

Tuesday, in Mark's account of events, begins at Mark 11:20, with its reference to 'in the morning', when it is discovered that the fig tree, cursed the previous day, has in fact withered. This is the last indication of time in Mark's Gospel before Mark 14:1 (see the note at the end of this chapter). A reading of Mark 11:20 through to the end of Mark chapter 13 gives the impression that not only the whole series of confrontations between Jesus and his critics, but also the discourse delivered on the Mount of

Olives, all took place on one and the same day. It is, of course, possible that these events stretched over *more* than one day. But on the basis that Mark has chosen to give us clear chronological markers up to the beginning of the Tuesday, the inference is that everything from Mark 11:20 to Mark 13:37 belongs to one and the same day.

It is at this point that we move from a fair degree of certainty about timing to informed guesswork.

Matthew and Luke do not provide indications of time, except for Matthew 21:17–18, and the reference to 'in the morning' in the second of these two verses is deliberately vague about which morning is being referred to, as Matthew—for editorial reasons—compresses the account of the cursing of the fig tree and the discovery of its actual withering into a single unit. Matthew includes material which is not found in either Mark or Luke—in particular (a) two additional parables that form part of Jesus' response to the challenge to his authority (Matt. 21:28–32 and 22:1–14); (b) Jesus' pronouncement of 'woes' on the scribes and Pharisees (Matt. 23:1–36); (c) Jesus' lament over Jerusalem (Matt. 23:37–39); and (c) a series of three sections which have to do with Jesus' Second Coming (Matt. 25:1–46). While we cannot be absolutely sure, a reading of these chapters most naturally leads to the supposition that chapter 23 follows on immediately from Jesus' teaching at the end of chapter 22 and that chapter 25 follows on directly from chapter 24. In other words, the working assumption is that all this extra material in Matthew also belongs to the Tuesday.

The case has been made so far for there being three days during which the events in Jesus' ministry in Jerusalem took place, at least with regard to those events recorded in the Synoptic Gospels. However, attention should be drawn to Luke 19:47 and 21:37, where we are told that Jesus was teaching in the temple 'daily' (in the former verse) and 'every day' (in the latter verse), so it may be that the teaching (and debating) discussed above was spread over more days than can be deduced directly from the text—or it may be that there was other teaching of Jesus on each day during this period of time which is not recorded in the Gospels.

In *John*'s Gospel we find an account of Jesus' activity in Jerusalem which takes place between the Triumphal Entry and Jesus washing his disciples' feet on the Thursday evening. This activity, recorded in John 12:20–50, begins with some Greeks wishing to meet Jesus, which leads to Jesus' words about his approaching death. That is followed by a comment by John on the unbelief of so many and a statement by Jesus about his role as the Saviour of the world. We do not know at which point during Jesus' time in Jerusalem the events recorded by John took place. There are no clues to work on. But, simply on the basis that the Sunday to Tuesday are occupied by the events recorded in Matthew, Mark and Luke, the guess is being made here (and it is no more than a guess) that John 12:20–50 belongs to the *Wednesday*.

The assumption is being made that none of the events recorded by any of the four Gospel writers took place on the *Thursday* until the accounts in all four Gospels of the meal in the Upper Room on the evening of that day—with the exception of Jesus giving instructions to his disciples at some point during that day, 'the day of Unleavened Bread', to make preparations for the Passover meal (Matt. 26:17–19; Mark 14:12–16; Luke 22:7–13). But this assumption can be no more than conjecture. We simply do not know whether Jesus spent the Thursday morning and afternoon in meditation and prayer as preparation for his approaching Passion, or whether some of the action assigned in this study to the Tuesday and Wednesday—or further teaching in the temple area—took place on that day.

A comment on the Gospel writers as reporters
It will be evident that in the accounts of these few days there are differences between the Gospel writers. As noted earlier, John's account is independent of Matthew, Mark and Luke. But it is the differences

between these three Synoptic writers which critics sometimes seize upon in order to suggest that the Gospel writers are unreliable. It will be helpful to examine this area a little further, in order to have a better understanding of the work of the Gospel writers. But we can be assured that none of the so-called discrepancies is of major significance, and to suggest the contrary amounts to nitpicking.

The differences between Matthew's, Mark's and Luke's accounts include examples of the following:

- On occasions, one or other writer includes material that is omitted by another (or both of the others). To give just one example, Matthew includes five units of teaching (mainly parables) in his narrative that are not found in Mark or Luke. There must have been a vast amount of material available to each of the Gospel writers, but each one had to be selective in his choice of incidents to be included. The very last verse of John's Gospel makes exactly this point: 'Now there are also many other things that Jesus did. Were every one of them to be written, I suppose that the world itself could not contain the books that would be written' (John 21:25).

- An incident may be recorded by one writer as taking place at a different point in the narrative from where it is placed by another. One example of this is commented on in the note at the end of this chapter. We need to recognize the role of the Gospel writers as editors of the material available to them. As stated in the chapter endnote, they did not always regard chronological accuracy as the most important consideration. This is not to accuse them of deliberately misrepresenting the facts: it is merely to acknowledge that these careful and conscientious writers sometimes judged that a change of strict chronological order would be the ideal way to intensify the focus on a particular aspect of what was happening. One further example of this may appear to be Jesus' lament over

Jerusalem, which Matthew records immediately after his account of Jesus' condemnation of the scribes and Pharisees (Matt. 23:37–39). Luke, however, reports that Jesus spoke very similar words at an earlier point in his ministry while still making his way towards Jerusalem (Luke 13:34–35). It is possible that Matthew deliberately placed authentic words of Jesus from some time earlier, expressing deep compassion for those people of Jerusalem, at this point in his Gospel in order to show Jesus' tenderness alongside his words of judgment. The combination of Jesus' authority and tenderness in this section of the Gospel narrative has already been commented on. Luke tells us that Jesus did indeed speak words of lament over Jerusalem during this time in the city, as recorded in Luke 19:41–44 (expressed differently from Luke 13:34–35). Luke places these words between the Triumphal Entry and the cleansing of the temple. Another possibility is, of course, that Jesus spoke the same (or similar) words on more than one occasion, just as many a preacher will make use of the same (or similar) material on different occasions, so that the correct 'solution' may be that the three sections (in the chronological order of Luke 13:34–35; Luke 19:41–44; and Matthew 23:37–39) each come at exactly the right place in the narrative!

• One or other Gospel writer may at times compress actions or spoken utterances that took place over a longer period of time, so that they appear to occupy a shorter period of time. One example of this has been referred to above, namely Matthew's account of the cursing of the fig tree, which may appear to suggest that the withering took place immediately, whereas Mark spells out for us that the tree was cursed on one day and the fact of its withering was discovered on the following day. Matthew is not contradicting Mark: he has edited his material by compressing the whole episode into a single unit.

- Jesus expresses himself in different words in the different accounts of what must be the same speech. Many examples of this are to be found in these passages. But it would be a mistake to suppose that any one version of a speech by Jesus must represent his *ipsissima verba* (the precise words he used). That would be impossible, as Jesus spoke in Aramaic and the Gospels provide a Greek translation. Again, we need to be mindful of the role of the Gospel writers as editors of the material available to them. At times they give their individual selections and translations, using a common source or independent sources. At times, one or other (and particularly Luke) gives a briefer summary; at other times one or other (and particularly Matthew) records at greater length.

- Words reported as being spoken by Jesus in one Gospel may be attributed to a different speaker in another Gospel. For example, in Mark's account of the Parable of the Tenants it is Jesus who answers his own question, 'What will the owner of the vineyard do?' by saying, 'He will come and destroy the tenants and give the vineyard to others' (Mark 12:9), whereas in Matthew's account Jesus poses the question and his hearers supply the answer: 'He will put those wretches to a miserable death and let out the vineyard to other tenants who will give him the fruits in their season' (Matt. 21:41). There is no problem here, of course. It takes little imagination to picture the scene: Jesus telling his parable, encouraging his listeners to engage in some verbal interaction and at the same time repeating the obvious point that has been voiced by one or more persons in the crowd.

So, to sum up the foregoing discussion, the alleged differences are of minor importance. In a court of law, reliable witnesses give their separate accounts of an incident or a conversation. Each one is equally truthful but there will almost certainly be differences in their statements, none of them invalidating the account of any of the others and each of them complementing the others.

Jesus' previous visits to Jerusalem

Another question should be addressed in this introduction: had Jesus visited Jerusalem on an earlier occasion before his final week of ministry? If we had only the Synoptic Gospels to look at, our answer would have to be 'No' (or 'Probably not')—with the exception, of course, of Jesus' presentation as a baby in the Jerusalem temple and his visit to Jerusalem as a twelve-year-old, both of these occasions being recorded only by Luke (Luke 2:22ff., 41ff.). But when we examine John's Gospel, it becomes apparent that Jesus had visited the capital on at least three earlier occasions in his adult years. These visits are referred to in the following verses, each introducing a period of ministry in Jerusalem: John 2:13 (continuing to 3:22); John 5:1 (continuing to the end of the chapter); John 7:10 (possibly continuing until 10:40—unless John 10:22 marks the beginning of a separate visit to Jerusalem).

Armed with this information, we can recognize clues in the Synoptic Gospels that point to earlier visits to Jerusalem. Mark mentions the sense of foreboding and dread on the part of the disciples when Jesus embarked on his final journey towards Jerusalem (Mark 10:32), which would imply that Jesus had spent time in the capital earlier and could expect fierce opposition from the Jewish leaders. A further clue is found in Luke's account of Jesus' visit to the home of Martha and Mary (Luke 10:38–42). While it is John who tells us that this home was in Bethany and that the two sisters and their brother Lazarus were special friends of Jesus (John 11:1, 5), Luke was no doubt aware of previous visits to this home, which—given its close proximity to Jerusalem—are likely to have included time spent in the capital. Jesus' ability to locate an ass (Mark 11:1ff.) and to make arrangements for the use of a furnished upper room

(Mark 14:12–16) are easier to understand if Jesus had various contacts in the vicinity of Jerusalem from previous visits there.

This discussion may well prompt the question as to why the Synoptic Gospels are so strangely silent about Jesus' earlier ministry in Jerusalem. The answer almost certainly has to do with the editorial purpose of each of the Gospel writers. Each of them has chosen, in the earlier part of his Gospel, to focus mainly on Jesus' ministry in Galilee and in neighbouring Gentile territory, and to reserve any account of Jesus' ministry in Jerusalem for the later part of his narrative, in order to highlight all the more emphatically what we might describe as Jesus' 'journey to the cross'. A brief comment on aspects of each Gospel writer's editorial purpose may be helpful to develop this link for each of the Synoptic writers between the cross and Jerusalem:

- *Mark's Gospel*, which may well be the earliest Gospel to have been written, is a Gospel of two halves. Part 1 (from the start of the Gospel until 8:30) asks the question *'Who is Jesus?'* Jesus provides many demonstrations of his authority over disease, demons, sin and death; his authority to call people to follow him; and his authority in teaching. Jesus can do what only God can do. Despite the persistent blindness on the part of his disciples to 'see' who Jesus is, he graciously opens their spiritual eyes, just as he has opened the physical eyes of a blind man, and Peter is enabled to affirm, 'You are the Christ' (Mark 8:29). Part 2 (from 8:31 until the end of the Gospel) asks the question *'What sort of Christ is Jesus?'* The answer spelt out again and again is that Jesus is the Christ who must suffer and die, in order to be the Saviour—the key verse being 10:45: 'For even the Son of Man came not to be served but to serve, and to give his life as a ransom for many.' Within this overall framework, it suited Mark's purposes to locate the action of Part 1 in Galilee and elsewhere in the north, and in Part 2 to show Jesus making his way towards Jerusalem and the cross.

- *Matthew's Gospel* interleaves sections of Jesus' teaching (e.g. the Sermon on the Mount in chapters 5–7 or parables in chapter 13) and sections of Jesus in action. But Matthew follows Mark's general approach of linking Jesus' time in Jerusalem to the final week of Jesus' ministry leading to the cross, in order to emphasize that this was the goal towards which the whole of Jesus' ministry was leading.
- *Luke's Gospel* makes the most pronounced use of the 'journey' motif. From 9:51, Luke develops what is sometimes called his 'travel narrative'. In this verse, Luke tells us, 'When the days drew near for him to be taken up, he set his face to go to Jerusalem.' From here on, the narrative is punctuated by references to the ongoing journey; for example, 'Now as they went on their way . . .'; 'He went on his way through towns and villages, teaching and journeying towards Jerusalem' (Luke 10:38; 13:22).

For the sake of completeness, a brief comment on the 'editorial purpose' of John's Gospel is also included, with particular reference to Jerusalem and the cross:

- *John's Gospel* (like Mark) is a Gospel of two halves. It has been described as a Passion narrative with an introduction. The introduction is chapters 1–12, and the Passion narrative (together with the closing parts of the Gospel) is chapters 13–21 (from Maundy Thursday evening onwards). The shadow of the cross covers the whole book, not only the second half. While John does not hold back from recording Jesus' earlier ministry in Jerusalem, as we have seen, he keeps the theme of the cross constantly in the reader's full view, particularly through recurring references to Jesus' 'hour', meaning the time of his atoning death (e.g. John 2:4; 7:30), and through a whole number of other pointed remarks which anticipate the cross (e.g. John 1:29; 3:14–15).

Prayer

Lord Jesus Christ,

You are THE LIVING WORD of the Father, who has caused the Bible to be written for our instruction and encouragement.

We thank you for the four Gospel writers and the accuracy of their records.

We thank you for your coming into this world to be our Saviour and for your determination to make your last journey to Jerusalem in order to go to the cross for our sakes.

We pray that our study of the final days of your public ministry will lead us to a greater understanding of your authority and your compassion, and to a closer walk with you day by day. Amen.

NOTE

1 Matthew and Mark record this event (without mentioning Mary by name) as an act of devotion that contrasts with the plotting of the Jewish leaders and with Judas's plan to betray Jesus, and they place this whole episode a little later in their accounts: immediately before the Passover meal that Jesus shares with his disciples (see Matt. 26:1–16 and Mark 14:1–11). The impression may therefore be given that Jesus' anointing at Bethany took place later in the week and should therefore be discussed in this study.. That is not in fact so and is a misunderstanding of what Matthew and Mark record. The only indication of time in either of those passages appears in Mark 14:1: 'It was now two days before the Passover and the Feast of Unleavened Bread.' This marker of time refers to the plotting by the chief priests and scribes, not to the dinner in Bethany. Chronological sequence was not the primary concern for any of the Gospel writers, and it makes sense to understand both Matthew and Mark placing their accounts of the act of devotion to Jesus at this slightly later position in their Gospels for the literary reason given at the beginning of this note. Luke does not record this anointing at Bethany at all. His account of a woman from off the streets anointing Jesus at a Pharisee's house (Luke 7:36–50) has to do with an entirely different incident, which would appear to have taken place earlier in Jesus' ministry.

The coming of the King

(MATTHEW 21:1–11; MARK 11:1–11; LUKE 19:28–44; JOHN 12:12–19)[1]

The long-expected King

Expectations ran high during the time of Jesus' ministry that God would send his King to deliver his people, as they had done for a long period of time before then. This King was identified as the 'Messiah', or 'Christ'. Both terms mean the 'Anointed One' and derive respectively from the Hebrew and the Greek.

The Old Testament fuelled these expectations. For example, immediately after Adam and Eve's disobedience in the Garden God promised that a deliverer would come who would defeat the serpent (Gen. 3:15). God's promise to Abraham that he would make him and his posterity a blessing to 'all the families of the earth' carried messianic implications (Gen. 12:1–3). Jacob, on his deathbed, pronounced a blessing on his son Judah that 'the sceptre shall not depart from Judah' (Gen. 49:10). This reference to the Messiah as a king took on fresh significance centuries later, when David (from the tribe of Judah) was anointed king, and particularly when God promised David that his house would last 'for ever' (2 Sam. 7:12–14). Here was a promise that pointed forward to the coming of someone who would reign as a greater David and would be known as God's Son. This promise became even more focused in Psalm 2, where 'the LORD' and 'his Anointed' are linked together. God announces, 'As for me, I have set my King on Zion, my holy hill', and the Christ responds, 'I will tell of the decree: The LORD said to me, "You are my Son; today I have begotten you"' (Ps. 2:6–7).

Therefore, when Jesus made his entry into Jerusalem on the Sunday of the final week of his ministry, he was announcing that all these expectations were fulfilled in him. The incomparably momentous nature of this event is underlined by the fact, already noted, that the Triumphal Entry is the only incident in the period of time covered by this study to be recorded in all four Gospels.

A public declaration

As also noted in the Introduction, this was the first time in his ministry that Jesus gave a public demonstration of his identity as the Messiah-King. Up to this stage in his ministry, Jesus had been concerned for the most part to keep his identity under wraps. It is true that he had given demonstrations of his identity by his exercise of authority in many areas—an authority that unmistakably pointed to a divine origin. This was touched on in the comments in the Introduction about Mark's Gospel. On one occasion in his ministry, John the Baptist sent messengers from his prison cell to ask Jesus to confirm his identity: was he, or was he not, the Christ? Jesus replied by listing some of his deeds in terms borrowed from Isaiah which referred to the activity of the Messiah (Matt. 11:2–6; Luke 7:18–23). There were other occasions too when Jesus explicitly claimed to be the Christ (e.g. John 4:25–26). So the evidence was there for those who could recognize it. But Jesus often urged those who acknowledged him to be the Christ, or even individuals who had been healed by him, to keep quiet about it (e.g. Matt. 9:30; 17:9; Mark 1:43; 8:30). The reason for this enforced secrecy would seem to be that Jesus was aware of wrong expectations that were held by many concerning the Christ. He did not want to be identified as a political leader: a king who would challenge the Romans or Herod. We see this in his rapid withdrawal from the crowds following the feeding of the five thousand, when people wanted to make him king (John 6:15). Nor did Jesus want to be labelled primarily as a healer. Jesus preferred to refer to himself as the 'Son of Man'. This term, borrowed from the Old Testament, was deliberately ambiguous. It could appear to imply ordinary humanity, as when the term appears in Ezekiel (e.g. Ezek. 2:1).

Or, more significantly, it could imply both humanity and divine authority, as in the use of this term in one of Daniel's visions (Dan. 7:13–14). 'Son of Man' was not a term popularly associated with the Christ, so it did not carry unhelpful associations.

Another aspect of Jesus' true identity as the Christ, alongside his kingly authority, was his understanding of himself as the Servant, particularly the Suffering Servant of the book of Isaiah. Isaiah 53 pointed to his role as the one who would die a substitutionary death for the sins of his people. As we have seen in the Introduction, it was only when his disciples had acknowledged him to be the Christ that he could begin to teach them what sort of Christ he truly was: the Christ who must suffer and die (Mark 8:31). This was a lesson that they failed to understand until after the resurrection. It was, of course, not just the disciples who lacked this understanding—so too did the rest of the people.

The Triumphal Entry

This, then, is the background to Jesus' entry into Jerusalem on Palm Sunday, when he publicly declared himself to be the Messiah-King. Each of the Gospel writers quotes the crowd's acclamation from Psalm 118 (118:26), which (along with the previous five psalms) formed 'the great Hallel' (the word means 'praise') used at major Jerusalem feasts like the Passover, as on this occasion. Whether with the addition 'the King' (as in Luke) or 'the King of Israel' (as in John), or without (as in Matthew and Mark), the context makes the kingly associations plain.

Each of the Gospel writers draws attention to Jesus' authority. He issued his instructions to his disciples to go and fetch the colt, and they carried out their orders. We notice that, in Matthew, Mark and Luke, Jesus' instructions specifically refer to himself as 'the Lord'. His authority was such that he had complete control of the young donkey, which—as Mark tells us—had not been ridden before. Matthew adds the detail that the colt's mother was brought along as well, which no doubt helped settle the younger animal.[2] We are to recognize, from the very start of this section of the narrative, that Jesus was in complete control of the events leading up to the cross.

Jesus was not simply revealing himself as the King, but he was also making a statement about the nature of his kingship:

- He is *the King of peace*. Matthew and John specifically refer to Zechariah's prophecy, which Jesus was deliberately fulfilling. Zechariah had written that Zion's king would return—not, as might be expected, riding a war horse, but in peace on a donkey's colt (Zech. 9:9). Matthew's quotation from Zechariah specifically includes the 'humble' character of this King.

- He is *the King of David's line*. As Jesus rode, the crowd proclaimed him to be the Davidic King, sent by God.

- He is *the Redeemer King*. The Old Testament associated 'Zion's King' with the rescue of God's people—hence that title for Jesus being included in the specific quotation of Zechariah in Matthew and John. As King Jesus entered the city, people cried, 'Hosanna!', which means 'Save us!' or 'Save now!'—and this was entirely appropriate. The entry into Jerusalem was a picture of the return from exile with the ransomed of the Lord entering Zion with singing—and that picks up on well-known words from Isaiah 35 (35:10).

Distinctive contributions of each of the Gospel writers

Each of the Gospel writers contributes a different point to notice at the end of his account of this incident:

- *Matthew* records the spirit of enquiry among the crowd concerning who Jesus was. 'Who is this?' is a recurring motif in all four Gospels (e.g. Matt. 11:3; Mark 2:6; Luke 8:25; John 7:40–46— to give one example from each Gospel). The popular consensus was that he was 'the prophet Jesus'. If this was an identification of

Jesus with the Messiah-figure of whom Moses spoke in terms of a prophet whom God would raise up to be like him and to whom they should listen (Deut. 18:15, 18), this was an accurate assessment. If, however, Jesus was being viewed on the level of just another prophet (as people were reported as doing earlier, Matt. 16:14), they failed to recognize his identity.

- *Mark* alone tells us that Jesus did not immediately proceed to cleanse the temple. Instead, as he tells us, Jesus looked at the temple and retired to Bethany for the night. There is an ominous note about all this: Jesus came as the judge, collecting evidence and adjourning court until the next morning.
- *Luke* records the hostility displayed by some of the Pharisees in the crowd because of the exuberant acclaim on the part of Jesus' supporters. Matthew includes a similar encounter in connection with the events of the following day. Such responses from Jesus' critics prepare us for the series of challenges that would take place later, mainly on the Tuesday (if the earlier discussion of the chronology is correct). They prepare us too for the cross of Good Friday.
- *John* comments on the disciples' failure to understand the significance of Jesus' entry into Jerusalem as King. Only after the cross and resurrection would understanding come. John too hints at the growing hostility of the Pharisees. Their comment about 'the world' having gone after Jesus is meant as an ironical comment on John's part. 'The world' are those whom Jesus has come to save, and God's purpose is that many should follow (or 'go after') his Son. The Pharisees, however, do not make the comment in that sense![3]

The material that John includes in the rest of his chapter 12 does not coincide at all with any of the teaching or incidents that are recorded in Matthew, Mark or Luke. Whether or not the suggestion in the

Introduction is correct, that John's remaining material records what took place *after* the events of these few days in Jerusalem that are recorded in the other three Gospels, we shall not examine the rest of John chapter 12 until the final section of this study.

Prayer

Lord Jesus Christ,

You are THE MESSIAH, *promised from long ago as the one who would come to redeem your people.*

We thank you for the public demonstration on the first Palm Sunday of your majesty, yet humbly riding into Jerusalem on a donkey as the King of peace.

We want to echo the crowd's shouts of 'Hosanna to the Son of David! Blessed is he who comes in the name of the Lord! Hosanna in the highest!'

We thank you that, while you looked at the heart of the city with a Judge's scrutiny, you wept over that same city with a Saviour's tenderness.

We ask that we would honour you not only on our lips but in our lives, which willingly submit to your kingly rule. Amen.

NOTES

1 For all the Scripture passages examined in each chapter, please refer to the appropriate 'Chapter' in the Appendix, where the passages are set out in full.

2 Some critics find fault with Matthew's account, as if, by referring to two animals, he has misunderstood the parallelism of Zechariah's prophecy, which refers to a single animal. But Matthew had a better grasp of Hebrew than his critics imagine. Similarly, when Matthew says that Jesus 'sat on them', some critics accuse him of a further misunderstanding, as if he imagined that Jesus sat on both animals. But the 'them' in Matt. 21:7 refers to the cloaks laid on the colt.

3 In Chapter 12 of this study there will be further discussion about 'the world', which is a major theme in John 12.

The fig tree and the temple

(Matthew 21:12–22; Mark 11:12–25; Luke 19:45–48)

The two strands of the narrative: the cursing of the fig tree and the cleansing of the temple

Mark's account is the one that is most concerned with providing a precise chronology of the cursing of the fig tree and the cleansing of the temple. As noted in the Introduction, it is only Mark who specifically tells us that the cleansing of the temple did not take place on the Sunday but on the Monday. It is only he who tells us that the action concerning the fig tree occurred over two days: the Monday and the Tuesday. As we have seen already, Matthew obviously compresses the action in his account. Luke devotes only four verses to the cleansing of the temple and its aftermath, and omits the incident of the fig tree altogether.[1]

The two main events in these verses in Mark and Matthew—the cursing of the fig tree and the cleansing of the temple—are closely connected, so that they each interpret the other. Matthew makes the connection by focusing first on the cleansing of the temple and then on the cursing of the fig tree. He lays them both out separately, one after the other, and expects his readers to make the connection for themselves. Mark deliberately interleaves the accounts of the two events in these verses and thereby emphasizes their link with each other. What will have been more obvious to the original readers than it may be to us is that the cursing of the fig tree is an acted parable, because they would have recognized the fig tree as a symbol of Israel (e.g. Hosea 9:10; Micah 7:1–6). So, far from the cursing of the fig tree being, as some have misunderstood it to be, a gratuitous act of ill-temper on Jesus' part, both the cursing of the fig tree and Jesus' action of cleansing the temple have to do with judgment on Israel.

Let us look in more detail at how this twofold judgment theme works out in Mark's account. It will help to set this out as a series of steps:

- *Step 1*. We have to go back to verse 11 of Mark 11 for this first step, where Jesus *looked at the temple*. He examined the evidence, as we have noted earlier.

- *Step 2*. Jesus *looked at the fig tree*—and also he *condemned the fig tree* in verses 12–14. In the Old Testament God looked for early spiritual fruit from the fig tree of Israel—he was hungry for that fruit. In this acted parable involving an actual fig tree, Jesus did exactly the same. Normally, leaves do not appear on a fig tree until after the fruit; so when he saw leaves, he had every reason to expect figs. But occasionally a 'precocious' fig tree produces leaves before the fruit season. So, when Jesus found this sort of tree, which appeared good but failed in its purpose, he condemned it.

- *Step 3*. Jesus *condemned the temple* in verses 15–19. Jesus went to the temple and carried out judgment—overturning the tables of the money-changers and the seats of the pigeon-sellers. It is possible—as is often said—that the money-changers (requiring people to use special temple coinage) charged exorbitant rates of exchange. It is possible too that the market obstructed prayer in the 'court of the Gentiles' (an area designated for non-Jewish worshippers to come a certain distance into the temple precincts). We cannot be absolutely sure, but these are reasonable assumptions. The *real* problem concerning the Jerusalem temple was that the religious activities which it engaged in were only 'leaves'. The fruit for which God was 'hungry' was missing.

All three Synoptic Gospel writers record Jesus' twofold accusation of those responsible for what happened in the temple. To quote from Mark 11:17, 'Is it not written, "My house shall be called a house of prayer for all the nations"? But you have made it a den of robbers.' The words used are quotations from Isaiah and Jeremiah (Isa. 56:7; Jer. 7:11). There may, or may not, have been dishonesty in the currency exchange and sale of stock. But the real problem was that they robbed God of the trust and obedience due to him, and they used the temple as a cover for godlessness. They neglected prayer and they failed to reach out to the nations (the Gentiles). They thought that, provided they kept the sacrificial system going, they could do as they liked, and it would not matter. What the temple consisted of—just like the fig tree—was religious show. The authorities carried out all the outward routines but there was no inward spiritual reality. Jesus was 'hungry' not simply for figs, but for the spiritual fruit which he, as their King, had every right to expect.

Compassion and grace for the disadvantaged

Only Matthew records Jesus' act of healing blind and lame people in the temple precincts immediately after his cleansing of the temple. It would seem that not only Gentiles but also those with physical disabilities were being prevented from entering the temple area and offering sacrifices. Jesus' miraculous act of compassion and grace to the disadvantaged was a significant challenge to any such restriction. Similarly, Matthew records that children (another disadvantaged group in society) were being rebuked for shouting words of praise, but Jesus defended their right to utter praise in the same way that he had supported his disciples' acclaim on the previous day in Luke's account (Luke 19:37–40). Here he quoted Psalm 8:2 as a basis for the appropriateness of the children's praise. Significantly, on both occasions, Jesus was in effect affirming that those praising him as the Messiah-King (or 'the Son of David') were right to do so. As Jesus had announced on an earlier occasion, 'something greater than the temple is here' (Matt. 12:6).

Further teaching on judgment

By clearing the temple, Jesus was passing judgment on Israel, particularly its religious leadership. But at this stage he was not carrying out the sentence. He was 'teaching' them (to use Mark's word in Mark 11:17).

So far, there has been a balance in the three steps of the action:

- Jesus looked at the temple.
- Jesus looked at the fig tree and condemned it.
- Jesus condemned the temple.[2]

However, there is a *Step 4* in the recorded action. We discover that sentence had been carried out on the fig tree. The fig tree had withered. Matthew, compressing the incident of the fig tree into a single event recorded in just three verses, is concerned to show the awful reality of the fate of the fig tree and does so by telling us twice that the fig tree withered 'at once'. Mark leaves open the question of when exactly the withering took place. Instead he tells us that it had occurred by the morning of the following day. Mark emphasizes the awful reality of the fig tree's destruction by telling us that it had 'withered away to its roots'. But the important point that Mark wants to convey by his concern for chronology is that *sentence had been carried out on the fig tree—but after a delay*.[3]

If we have followed the logic of these four steps, spelt out by Mark, we have to ask ourselves what this means for the temple. Notice was being given that there would be a *Step 5*. The answer must be: *sentence would be carried out on the temple—but after a delay*. Once Jesus condemned the temple, the axe hovered over it until the cross. Then it too, just like the fig tree, would wither and die, starting with the roots, but including the now-so-impressive leaves. When Jesus died on the cross as the sacrifice to end all sacrifices, the sacrificial system of the temple became obsolete—once for all. That would be demonstrated in the account of Jesus' crucifixion, when the curtain in the temple was supernaturally torn in two at the moment when Jesus died. The death of Jesus secured access to God for those who trust in him. Furthermore, the historical reality is that, forty years later, the Romans utterly destroyed Jerusalem, including the temple.

Chapter 2

One cleansing of the temple, or two?

One further question concerning Jesus' cleansing of the temple needs to be addressed, and that concerns the relationship between the Synoptic Gospel writers and John in their reporting of this incident. John records a cleansing of the temple at the beginning of Jesus' ministry (John 2:14–17). Matthew, Mark and Luke record Jesus' cleansing of the temple here towards the end of his ministry. Many writers assume that there can only have been one such action in the temple and discuss whether it is the Synoptics or John who place the incident in its 'correct' chronological slot, assuming that it is the other(s) who has relocated the incident for editorial purposes. But a case can be made for there having been two separate cleansings of the temple. The Synoptics' decision, discussed in the Introduction, not to record Jesus' earlier ministry in Jerusalem would account for them not referring to the earlier cleansing, which John does include. John's decision not to record the later cleansing of the temple is not evidence in itself that it did not take place. Both John and the Synoptics give every appearance of claiming to be concerned with setting their respective accounts in a precise chronological framework, and this natural reading of the texts should not be dismissed lightly. It may be significant that, in John's *early* cleansing of the temple, there is no reporting of a conspiracy by the religious authorities to have Jesus arrested and killed, when Jesus at this time would not have established his reputation, whereas the *later* cleansing, recorded by the Synoptics, most certainly appears to have been a major factor in galvanizing the Jerusalem hierarchy into taking decisive action against Jesus.

It may also be significant, in the discussion of this question, that it is John—in his reporting of the *early* cleansing—who records Jesus' words to those who challenged him on that occasion: 'Destroy this temple, and in three days I will raise it up.' John goes on to explain that Jesus was speaking about the temple of his body and was anticipating his resurrection (John 2:18–22). Matthew, Mark and Luke, by contrast, do not record this saying of Jesus in connection with the *later* cleansing of the temple. But Matthew and Mark do record that a garbled version of Jesus' words was used against him at his trial before the Sanhedrin (Matt. 26:61; Mark 14:58). It is reasonable to suggest that, if Jesus had made this statement on the occasion of his cleansing of the temple on the day after Palm Sunday, Matthew and/or Mark would have made that connection clear. It is also reasonable to suggest that they did not do so because they knew that Jesus' words about the temple belonged to the earlier incident, which they chose not to record.

Faith, prayer and forgiveness (Matt. 21:21–22; Mark 11:22–25)

Both Matthew and Mark record a statement by Jesus on the subject of *faith* in response to the disciples' surprise at the discovery of the withering of the fig tree. In each of these two Gospels, Jesus goes on to make a statement too about *prayer*. And in Mark alone there is a further statement by Jesus on the subject of *forgiveness*.[4] This little section of teaching is very brief, and while each of the two (or three) statements encapsulates a key principle about Christian living, the development of thought through these few verses, so as to make a progression from one to the other, and the reason for the inclusion of these three statements at this point of the narrative, may not be altogether obvious.

One possible way to understand the purpose of these verses being included here is to regard them as Jesus' commentary on the preceding events. Peter (in Mark's account) and the disciples collectively (in Matthew) were understandably shocked at what had happened to the fig tree. We can take it that they would have begun to take on board (either at this point in time or through earlier teaching) that the fig tree represented Israel and that the heart of the nation was tied up with the temple. But now they had been told that the temple and the sacrificial system were under judgment. That being the case, it would be natural for them to be asking such questions as 'If the temple and the sacrificial system disappear, how will anyone be ransomed or atoned for? How will anyone get into the kingdom if Israel is going to be condemned?'

Whatever precisely was going through the disciples' minds, Jesus focused their attention on three things:

- First, there is his statement about *faith*. Jesus' point may be that, in view of the sobering truth that judgment would fall on the temple and on those involved in its bad practices, it is important not to trust in religious observance, however impressive it may be. Rather, they should trust in God—he is the one they should have faith in. The figure of a mountain being thrown into the sea is one that Jesus had used earlier to refer to a miracle. He had said that even 'faith like a grain of mustard seed' (but, from the context, a faith that looks to God) can bring about miracles (Matt. 17:20). There is no obstacle—not even the removal of the temple from religious life—that can thwart God's purposes.

- Second, Jesus' statement about *prayer*. Jesus said that God can do the seemingly impossible for those who seek him trustingly, and— if this is indeed a response to the disciples' shock at the demise of the temple—God can bring about the salvation of anyone. Therefore, when you ask God for the humanly impossible thing you need, and specifically salvation from judgment, you are not to trust in anything *you* do, but rather to trust in what *he* has done.

- Third, Jesus' words (in Mark) about *forgiveness*. In the context of concerns about salvation and judgment, to have faith in God and to pray believingly mean admitting that you are a forgiven sinner. Therefore, because you have been forgiven, this must mean forgiving others.

Prayer

Lord Jesus Christ,

You are THE JUDGE, *before whose eyes nothing is hidden and the secrets of all hearts are revealed.*

We ask for your mercy when we fail to produce the fruit of trust and obedience in our lives and are more concerned with the outward display of leaves.

We ask for genuine faithfulness in our daily lives: for greater consistency between what we profess and what we are.

We thank you that, even in the process of your activity as Judge, you showed compassion and grace in Jerusalem then for the needy and for those who looked to you—and we thank you for your compassion and grace today.

We pray that you would increase our faith in your power to save; deepen our praying for your will to be done; and make us more willing to forgive others, as we ourselves have been forgiven. Amen.

NOTES

1　But see Luke 21:29–33, where Jesus draws a lesson from a fig tree. These words, which are reported by all three Synoptic writers, will be discussed in due course. See also note 3 below.

2　A number of times in his Gospel, Mark makes use of a threefold A-B-A structure, which can be compared to a 'sandwich' with two outside layers which balance each other (the two 'A's) and an inner filling (the 'B'). Normally there is either a contrast or a similarity between the content of the outer layers and the inner filling. One typical example is Mark 14:1–11, referred to in the note at the end of the Introduction, where the outer layers concern the theme of plotting (on the part of the chief priests and scribes, and Judas) in contrast to the theme within the 'inner filling' of devotion (on the part of the woman of Bethany). Up to this point in Mark 11 we have a typical 'Marcan sandwich', but this one is somewhat more complex, because there is a further twist in the narrative, as the following verses show.

3 In Luke 13:6–9 Jesus tells a parable about a barren fig tree which is under sentence of being cut down but, despite three years of fruitlessness, is allowed another year of grace before the axe falls.

4 Mark 11:26 does not appear in several important manuscripts and is therefore omitted in most modern Bible versions. Where it is added (often in a footnote to the Bible text), it reads: 'But if you do not forgive, neither will your Father who is in heaven forgive you.' It is probable that the similarity of Mark 11:25 to Matt. 6:14 led to these extra words being added from Matt. 6.15 in some manuscripts.

Challenge 1: a question of authority

(MATTHEW 21:23–22:14; MARK 11:27–12:12; LUKE 20:1–18)

A series of conflicts

Each of the Synoptic Gospel writers continues with a series of conflict-episodes. Altogether there are five separate encounters. Matthew and Mark record all five, while Luke omits the fourth encounter (Jesus' conversation with a scribe—in other words, an expert in the Old Testament law). These five episodes are dealt with in this and the four following chapters of this study, with each one being labelled a 'challenge'. In each of the first four, Jesus' enemies seek to debate with him and ask him a trick question—and each time Jesus turns the tables and leaves them totally wrong-footed. In the fifth round of debating, it is Jesus who issues a challenge, to which his critics can offer no answer.

This chapter deals with the first challenge, which is the longest of the five in all three Synoptic Gospels. It is even longer in Matthew, because he alone includes two parables (in addition to the Parable of the Tenants) which form part of Jesus' response to his opponents.

We find Jesus teaching in the temple—Luke adds the words 'preaching the gospel'. Here is one of those tantalizing places in the Gospel narrative where we would love to know just what Jesus was saying, beyond the content that is recorded for us. There is no indication that it is recorded elsewhere in the Gospels.

The authority of Jesus challenged (Matt. 21:23–27; Mark 11:27–33; Luke 20:1–8)

Representatives of all three components of the Sanhedrin (the Jewish council) came to Jesus while he was teaching in the temple—the chief priests, the scribes (also known as the teachers of the law—the religious experts) and the elders. They wanted to know about the nature and the source of Jesus' authority. Following Jesus' extraordinary actions in the temple the previous day, they felt they had good cause to demand his credentials. But their enquiry was not an honest one. They were already intent on having Jesus killed, as we have been told earlier (Mark 11:18; Luke 19:47). But they wanted to find a plausible reason for doing it. Their cunning plan with their double question to Jesus was designed to force him either to make a claim to be the Messiah, which they would take straight to Pilate as evidence of insurrection, or to deny his authority and lose his popularity with the crowd: 'By what authority are you doing these things, and who gave you this authority?'

But Jesus replied with a brilliant counter-question: 'Was the baptism of John from heaven or from man?' If they were to answer Jesus' question correctly, they would in fact be answering their own too. John taught that the one who followed him would be the Lord, who would baptize with the Holy Spirit (fulfilling the prophecy of Ezekiel: Matt. 3:11; Ezek. 36:26–27). The authorities found that it was *they*, and not Jesus, who were stuck for a safe answer. If they said John *was* a prophet from God, Jesus would challenge them about their response to John's message. Then their only options would be either to acknowledge Jesus, which they refused to do, or openly to reject the word of God. But if they said John was *not* a prophet from God, they would lose the crowd.

The only answer they managed to come up with was, 'We do not know.' This was, of course, not only a lame answer; it was also dishonest. Jesus correctly took their answer to mean, 'We won't tell you', and he replied with 'Neither will I tell you by what authority I do these things.'

However, Jesus did go on to give his critics a reply, and in so doing he showed them the seriousness of their position. This was not a matter of indulging in an intellectual debate. Their spiritual destiny was at stake: if they failed to face up to the truth about Jesus' identity as King, and therefore his divine authority, they were condemning themselves to a lost eternity. Jesus' reply came in the form of three parables.

The Parable of the Two Sons (Matt. 21:28–32)

The first, found only in Matthew, is known as the Parable of the Two Sons. The father in the story obviously represents God. With the help of Jesus' own comment following the short story, the two sons can be identified as the tax collectors and prostitutes (the first son, who initially defied his father's command but later repented) and the leaders of Israel (the second son, who professed obedience but in fact failed to carry out the command).

God had spoken to his people loudly and clearly in the Old Testament Scriptures. That message can be summed up by the father's words in the story: 'Son, go and work in the vineyard today.' Three aspects of God's revelation of himself to his people stand out in these words:

- *A privilege to cherish.* The leaders of Israel stood in a privileged position before God. They should have known and valued the honour of being loved by God and being regarded as his family. While 'Father' is a name that Jesus has specifically taught us to call God, the Old Testament makes plain God's tenderness towards his people, so that they should know that he acts towards them as to a 'son' (e.g. Hosea 11:1, 3). These members of the religious hierarchy were well versed in the Old Testament Scriptures and had every opportunity to know the mind and will of God for themselves and those they were supposed to instruct and lead. More surprising is the implication from these words that 'the tax collectors and the prostitutes' should also be addressed by God as his 'son'. While God is altogether holy and 'of purer eyes than to see evil' (Hab. 1:13), he is also the God of grace, who longs to reach out to those who are disobeying him. Implicit here is the suggestion that these leaders of Israel, who opposed Jesus and regarded themselves as the custodians of God's law, should have shown a less judgmental attitude towards those who were far from God, and should have done more to win them back.

- *A command to obey.* To 'go and work in the vineyard' spells out God's purposes for his people. The vineyard, just like the fig tree, was a common Old Testament symbol of Israel.[1] We have already seen that God was hungry for fruit from his people, just as Jesus was hungry for spiritual fruit from the temple. Instead of their energies being expended on the externals of religious activity (just like the leaves of the fig tree, earlier), the leaders of Israel should have been cultivating the fruits of prayer and obedience and outreach to those far from God. They went through the motions of making the right noises. Their promises to obey sounded genuine enough. But the fact was that they failed to obey. In contrast, sinners—as represented by the tax collectors and prostitutes—had wandered far from God, but many had responded to John the Baptist, just as many had responded to Jesus (e.g. Luke 3:12; 5:27–32; 7:34, 36–50). Albeit belatedly, they had shown evidence of the fruit of repentance and faith in God.
- *An urgency to recognize.* The word 'today' spells out the urgency for his people of obeying God's mandate. While every day is a 'today', Jesus was surely applying that word to this very day on which he was challenging his opponents. Now, and not a moment later, was the time for them to face up to reality. They should repent and believe, just like the first son in the story.

The Parable of the Tenants (Matt. 21:33–46; Mark 12:1–12; Luke 20:9–18)

The next parable—the major part of Jesus' reply to his critics—is recorded by all three Synoptic Gospel writers. The Parable of the Tenants spells out what God will do to those who deny Jesus' authority.

It was noted in connection with the previous parable in Matthew that the vineyard was a common Old Testament symbol of Israel. Jesus' story carries strong echoes of a similar story about Israel as a vineyard that has gone wrong, to be found in Isaiah (Isa. 5:1–7). From that Old Testament story, Jesus' hearers would have had no problems in understanding the owner of the vineyard to represent God, the vineyard to be Israel and the missing fruit a little later in the story to be justice and righteousness. In this story, unlike the situation with the real fig tree a little earlier, it was the right time for the fruit, and the owner had a legal claim to it. All three Gospel writers record that the chief priests, elders and teachers of the law recognized themselves as the tenants in the story. As such, they were therefore answerable to God.

The servants whom the owner sent represent the Old Testament prophets, so many of whom Israel rejected, ill-treated and even killed. Finally, the owner sent his son. In an almost casual way, Jesus—who would have reckoned on his hearers interpreting for themselves the meaning of the story as he told it—was implicitly claiming to be the son—in other words, the Son of God. This was not the first time that Jesus had made such a claim (e.g. John 5:17ff.). In the story, the owner of the vineyard expected the tenants to respect his son. We, of course, know that, in the plan of God the Father, this would not happen. The divine plan was that Jesus would be put to death on the cross. But the telling of this part of the story invites our agreement that such rejection of the Son of God is astonishing. Jesus confronted the Jewish authorities with the enormity of what they were about to do. They knew that Jesus was God's Son, sent by God, and yet they planned to kill him. They thought they could have the temple without God. Their religion had become idolatry.

The consequence is judgment. The tenants left the owner of the vineyard out of their reckoning. The parallel in reality was that Israel mistakenly reckoned without God's power. They believed the old lie that there is no judgment. The tenants' punishment fits the crime: they are the ones to be thrown out of the vineyard and killed.

Israel was supposed to be a light to the nations, but they had not acted as such. But judgment on the unrepentant is coupled with grace to outsiders. What would happen now is that the vineyard would be 'given' (not 'let') to others. The gospel would go to all nations.

Jesus went on to quote from Psalm 118 (the same psalm that people were shouting on Palm Sunday) and he singled out verses which foretell the cross (Ps. 118:22–23). Jesus is the stone that the builders rejected, but he would become the 'cornerstone' (or 'the head of the corner')—and this was 'the Lord's doing'!

The sad ending of this incident is that Israel, represented by its leaders, refused to listen. They became even more determined to do away with Jesus. But we need to heed the warning that we similarly ignore the truth about judgment every time we sin.

The Parable of the Wedding Feast (Matt. 22:1–14)

Only Matthew includes this particular parable. It has some similarities with the Parable of the Great Banquet in Luke 14:16–24, but Luke specifically relates Jesus' telling of that parable to a Sabbath meal that Jesus attended at the home of a 'ruler of the Pharisees' (Luke 14:1, 15), while Matthew records that this parable was part of the debate between Jesus and his critics in his final week of ministry.

The story is one of warning to those whose hearts are hostile towards God and his Christ. It speaks powerfully of the grace of God to all who will receive it. Jesus was pleading with these men, who intended to have him killed, to respond to God's loving invitation before it was too late. While Jesus continued to warn unmistakably of judgment, as in the previous parable, there was still an opportunity for hard hearts to be softened by the love of God—just as today that opportunity is still available.

The parable contains two notes of warning.

The first is the warning *against refusing the invitation*. Jesus described heaven as a wedding feast. It is a picture of joy and celebration. The implication is that the king's son is the Messiah. The Old Testament refers to God as the husband of his people (e.g. Isa. 62:4–5; Hosea 2:16–20). Both here and elsewhere Jesus describes himself as the bridegroom, and that title for Jesus appears in other places too in the New Testament (Matt. 9:15; John 3:29; Eph. 5:25–32; Rev. 21:2, 9). God's invitation to the wedding feast went out loudly and clearly. It was common in those days for there to be a double invitation. Guests were both notified in advance, and also summoned when the feast was ready. The king in the story pleaded with his guests to come and spelt out for them the greatness of the banquet to which they were invited. One shock in the story is the trivial and selfish nature of the reasons given by the guests for refusing the invitation. An even greater shock is the mistreatment, even the murder, of some of the king's messengers by the invited guests. This part of the story echoes the action of the tenants in the previous story towards the vineyard owner's servants. But given that the king in this story, just like the owner in that previous story, represents none other than God himself, their hostile refusal of the invitation was a serious matter. The response of the king, in sending an army to destroy the murderers and to burn their city, was only to be expected.

Nevertheless, God's purpose is that heaven shall be full and that there shall be nothing lacking in the celebration of his Son's marriage. And so, just as in the previous story the vineyard was given to others, the invitation to the feast of heaven went out to all kinds of other people, as many as could be found, 'both bad and good'. The meaning of this part of the parable is that the invitation of the gospel would be extended to sinners and Gentiles, as many as would respond to the summons to repent and believe.

The second warning is *against ignoring the dress code*. In the story the guest at the feast who had no wedding garment faced the most awful judgment. This is, of course, a further shock in Jesus' story. Clothes serve as a pictorial representation of what a person is truly like.[2] The application for those of us who read this part of Scripture is that a person with proper wedding clothes is someone who has really responded to the gospel invitation. They have repented and believed, and so have received forgiveness and new life in Christ. We notice that the king in the story had not only provided the feast, but he had also provided the festal robes for his guests to wear.

By contrast, this individual without proper wedding clothes is someone who claims to be one of God's people but has *not* truly responded to Christ. He believes that his best is good enough for God. He believes that he can participate in the feast prepared for God's people without following the proper instructions. There has been no change of heart. The warning for Jesus' hearers, particularly the chief priests and the elders, was that outward religious observance by itself was not sufficient to make them acceptable to God. Nothing other than a humble admission that they had failed to honour Jesus as God's Son and a decisive calling on God for his mercy was what was required. The alternative prospect is set out in horrendous terms: Jesus' language here in 22:13 is that which he regularly used in his warnings of hell (see also Matt. 8:12; 13:42, 50; 24:51; 25:30). Jesus' hearers still had time to amend their ways, but time was fast running out. God, however, is sovereign in the matter of who will ultimately be present, or not be present, at the wedding feast of heaven. In Matthew's wording, 'many are called'—here in the sense of having the invitation of the gospel presented to them—'but few are chosen': ultimately, membership of the kingdom of heaven is a result of God's sovereign choice.

Malachi fulfilled

Before proceeding to Jesus' next encounter with his critics, we take a moment to consider that this part of the Gospel narrative represents a fulfilment of words of God spoken through Malachi:

Behold, I send my messenger, and he will prepare the way before me. And the Lord whom you seek will suddenly come to his temple; and the messenger of the covenant in whom you delight, behold, he is coming, says the LORD of hosts. But who can endure the day of his coming, and who can stand when he appears? (Mal. 3:1–2)

Two 'messengers' are spoken of here. The first is John the Baptist. He is the one who prepared the way for the Messiah's coming (Isa. 40:3; Matt. 3:3). The second is none other than the Messiah himself, described as 'the Lord' and 'the messenger of the covenant'. He is the one who would bring to completion God's promise (his covenant) to deliver his people. The close connection between the ministries of John the Baptist and Jesus has figured twice in this episode, both in Jesus' first response to the leaders of Israel and in his Parable of the Two Sons. At this point in the narrative, the Messiah had indeed come to his temple. His coming might be described as 'sudden' in that he gave no advance notice of his intention to clear the temple precincts of money-changers and traders. In addition, he had come to call people to account, as implied in Malachi's prophecy. The words in Malachi's prophecy 'whom you seek' and 'in whom you delight' are spoken sarcastically, because the people of his day—just like the spiritual leaders of Israel confronting Jesus—would have claimed to be orthodox and devout in their religious observance, and yet the reality was that their hearts were far from God and they were seeking to destroy their Messiah.

Prayer

Lord Jesus Christ,

You are THE SON OF GOD *with all authority from the Father in heaven and on earth.*

We thank you for your power to demolish all the arguments of those who oppose you.

We thank you that, although you were rejected by men, you have become the cornerstone.

We thank you for the privilege of being called by grace to be sons and daughters of God and to join in the wedding feast of heaven.

Help us to respond in repentance and faith—and to obey the command to go and work in your vineyard today. Amen.

NOTES

1   E.g. Ps. 80:8; Isa. 5:1. The cluster of grapes referred to in Num. 13:23–24, which was so large that it needed to be carried by two of the twelve spies who were sent into the Promised Land to reconnoitre the country, is an apt picture of the fruitfulness that was to characterize Israel: it has become the present logo of the Israeli Ministry of Tourism.

2   Another example of this can be found in Rev. 7:9, 13–14, where Christian believers are pictured as those who 'have washed their robes and made them white in the blood of the Lamb'.

Challenge 2: a question of allegiance

(MATTHEW 22:15–22; MARK 12:13–17; LUKE 20:19–26)

A surprising coalition

Following the substantial first round of the series of conflicts between Jesus and his critics, the second challenge is shorter but no less significant. The opponents who stepped forward on this occasion were the Pharisees and Herodians, as both Matthew and Mark tell us.[1] This was a most surprising coalition. The Pharisees were ultra-religious and the Herodians were ultra-secular. Under normal circumstances they would have had next to nothing in common. However, what brought them together as unlikely allies was their shared opposition to Jesus.[2]

A taxing question

The trick question that they had cooked up between themselves concerned the hated poll tax levied by the occupying power of Rome. Some people argued that, because the Roman coins bore an idolatrous inscription (referring to Caesar as a god), it was not 'lawful' to pay such taxes to Caesar. So the Pharisees and Herodians pretended to be on Jesus' side by overlaying their question with an incredibly thick coating of flattery.

As with the previous trick question, they reckoned that they had set an inescapable trap for Jesus, whichever way he answered. If he were to say, 'Yes, it is lawful to pay', he would alienate the crowd, and without the crowd around they could arrest him without there being a riot. If Jesus were to say, 'It is not lawful to pay', the Romans would arrest and kill him on charges of sedition.

One wonders if it never occurred to them that Jesus would see through their hypocrisy, as of course he did. As previously, he neutralized his opponents' question. His master stroke this time was to ask for a coin. Possibly, this in itself was an indication of Jesus' material poverty and would have set him apart from his more affluent opponents. The fact that *they* had to produce a coin immediately associated them with the use of the Roman currency, thus denying them the ability to act as if they had not already adopted a particular stance on this question: the implication is that they were perfectly happy to use the coinage and to pay the tax. Jesus then forced them to admit that Caesar's 'likeness and inscription' were on it, indicating that the coinage was not only guaranteed by Caesar but actually belonged to Caesar.

This gave Jesus the opening to make his celebrated (and profound) statement concerning the things that are Caesar's and the things that are God's. The first part of Jesus' statement was 'Render to Caesar the things that are Caesar's.' People obviously could not evade returning to Caesar what was his anyway. This was a statement of fact without any hint of adopting a political position. But then Jesus went on to the second part of his statement: 'And render to God the things that are God's.' 'Render'—in both parts of the statement—implies the repayment of a debt.

A challenge to our allegiance

It is important not to misunderstand the force of what Jesus was saying. He was not saying that we are to give some things to the state and that we are to give other things to God (or the church). It is always a mistake to imagine that we can divide our lives into different compartments and behave as if God has no rights in some of them. The second part of Jesus' command is actually far more challenging, and it constitutes the main part of his answer. He has already said that he is the Son of God who has come to claim what is due to God, and that those who murder him will be judged. Jesus has made the point that a coin is due to Caesar because it bears Caesar's image. But it is equally true that men and women bear God's image. That is a fundamental point from the account of creation (Gen. 1:26–27). That means that our whole life belongs to God and is due to him. Were the Pharisees and Herodians prepared for such a penetrating response to their question? Not at all. Jesus' answer faces every person in every age with a call to examine their response to God's sovereign claim on every area of their being.

If this challenge were not enough in itself, there was another one which Jesus' critics were not prepared to face up to. They were prepared to acknowledge that the coin they produced bore the 'image' of Caesar. But the one who was speaking to them was himself 'the image of God' (2 Cor. 4:4; Col. 1:15). By failing to honour the Son and by persisting in asking him trick questions, they were placing themselves in grave spiritual danger.

Ironically, Jesus' opponents 'marvelled' at Jesus' answer. All three Synoptic Gospel writers report this. Their trap had failed.

Prayer

Lord Jesus Christ,

You are THE IMAGE OF GOD and the exact imprint of the nature of God. You are the only God, who is at the Father's side, and you have made the Father known to us.

We thank you that we have been created in the image of God and belong to you.

We ask that we may acknowledge your Lordship over every part of our lives.

Help us, therefore, to live our lives faithfully as citizens on earth, but even more so as those with the higher calling of citizens of heaven. Amen.

Chapter 4

NOTES

1 Luke mentions only the scribes and the chief priests.

2 Mark records the origin of this alliance between Pharisees and Herodians in opposition to Jesus early in his ministry in Mark 3:6.

Challenge 3: a question of life and death

(Matthew 22:23–33; Mark 12:18–27; Luke 20:27–40)

A doctrinal challenge

The particular group of opponents who launched the third round of the contest with Jesus were the Sadducees. Each of the three Synoptic Gospel writers draws attention to the distinctive feature of the Sadducees' beliefs, namely that they did not believe in resurrection. This was in contrast to the Pharisees.[1] It would appear that the Sadducees regarded only the Pentateuch (the five books of Moses) as authoritative and on that basis they considered resurrection to be a belief that developed later.[2]

The Sadducees' question to Jesus was not as blatant as the earlier two, but it was nevertheless hostile. They used a parable with a sting in the tail, much as Jesus often did, and it appeared to show that the doctrine of resurrection (which the Sadducees did not believe in), when taken alongside undeniable scriptural truth, led to ridiculous conclusions. Their story was, of course, thoroughly contrived and relied heavily on the Old Testament principle of levirate marriage, which meant that, if a married man died childless, his next brother was obliged to marry his widow and raise up children to perpetuate the name of the deceased (Gen. 38:8; Ruth 1:11–13; 4:1–22).

The implication of the story was to discredit belief in resurrection, because in their view it could lead to great difficulties in terms of marriage relationships in the imagined after-life.

A warning against culpable ignorance

The Sadducees could imagine only two possible responses from Jesus.

They thought that he must either affirm resurrection and be made to look foolish, or deny resurrection and as a result antagonize the Pharisees still further. They did not expect Jesus to deliver his devastating demolition of their theological position. It is Matthew and Mark who include Jesus' withering comment that the Sadducees were 'wrong'. In Mark's account, Jesus not only began his response on this note but also concluded it in the same way. Jesus accused these men, who were considered to be theological experts, of being wrong on two counts. They were *ignorant of the Scriptures* and they were *ignorant of the power of God*. Jesus then developed those two points in reverse order.

First, they were *ignorant of the power of God*. What they failed to comprehend was that marriage is for this life only. If God has the power to resurrect, which indeed he has, he has power to change people in other ways. In heaven, people will not need to have children to carry on their name, because there will be no dying. No verse in the Old Testament tells us this in so many words, but the shock for these supposed theological experts was that Jesus was telling them exactly what heaven is really like. But he has the authority to do so, because he is the Son of God and heaven is where he has come from.

Second, they were *ignorant of the Scriptures*. It is significant that Jesus quoted to them from the book of Exodus about Moses and the burning bush (Exod. 3:1–6). After all, this incident came from the part of Scripture that they particularly revered. Jesus was invading their home territory and pointing out to them a truth that they had failed to recognize. The burning bush itself suggested eternal life because it was undestroyed by fire. Furthermore, if God could say, '*I am* the God of Abraham, and the God of Isaac, and the God of Jacob', when (physically) they had been dead for hundreds of years, and if God's nature is to redeem people from death, it is impossible that the patriarchs (Abraham, Isaac and Jacob) should be dead as far as God is concerned. Jesus effectively proved that the truth of resurrection is to be found in the first five books of the Bible.

Responses to Jesus

The concluding comments of Matthew's and Luke's accounts are significant. Luke tells us that some of the scribes were impressed by Jesus' reply to the Sadducees. No doubt they were Pharisees, who would have been delighted to see their theological rivals embarrassed. But the scribes were presented earlier as Jesus' enemies, so it is remarkable that they applauded Jesus. Matthew focuses here, as at the end of the previous encounter, on the crowd's astonishment at Jesus' teaching. Luke, in addition, makes the comment that Jesus' critics no longer dared to ask him any question, because—in Luke's narrative—this is the last challenge to Jesus from the hierarchy. Matthew and Mark reserve a similar comment until slightly later in their accounts (Matt. 22:46; Mark 12:34).

Prayer

Lord Jesus Christ,

You are THE RESURRECTION AND THE LIFE. You are the Living One who died and is alive for evermore.

We thank you for the certainty of life beyond the grave for all who put their trust in you.

We ask that you would assure us of your power to transform our lowly bodies to be like your glorious body.

We ask you also to help us grow in our knowledge of the Bible and our commitment to follow its teaching. Amen.

NOTES

1 Paul, on trial before the Jewish Sanhedrin, made use of this fundamental difference of belief between Sadducees and Pharisees in Acts 23:6–9.

2 For the Pharisees, such texts as Isa. 26:19 and Dan. 12:2 pointed to resurrection.

Challenge 4: a question of importance

(MATTHEW 22:34–40; MARK 12:28–34)

A comparison of Matthew, Mark and Luke

There are significant differences between Matthew's and Mark's reporting of this encounter, but they are by no means irreconcilable.

Matthew's focus is on the Pharisees as a group in their opposition to Jesus. Following Jesus' undisputed victory over the Sadducees, the Pharisees conferred together and set up one of their number to ask Jesus a question with the aim of 'testing' him. This indicates hostile intent. Presumably the expectation was to find fault with Jesus' answer to the question about which was the 'great [or most important] commandment in the Law'. As a result, they hoped to discredit Jesus and do harm to his reputation.

Mark's focus is on the individual who asked the question. Matthew has described him as a 'lawyer', and Mark calls him a 'scribe'. Both terms mean much the same thing, namely an expert in the study of the Old Testament law. While Mark's account may give the impression that the man acted on his own initiative, this cannot have been the full story in the light of what Matthew tells us. He must have been keen to ask Jesus the question, and we can imagine that he managed to persuade the Pharisees to allow him to be the one to do so. He may well have had some doubts about Jesus, but Mark goes out of his way to show us that this man, as an individual, was not a hostile critic, even though the group for whom he was acting as the mouthpiece were bitterly opposed to Jesus. When Mark says that he 'came' and 'heard', and then describes the man as 'seeing' that Jesus answered well, he uses three words which he has used earlier in his Gospel of people who have approached Jesus in the right way. So, although he was not a disciple, he displayed all the signs of someone who wanted to know more.

Luke omits this encounter altogether. The reason for the omission may be that Luke had already included Jesus' meeting with a different lawyer who likewise asked Jesus a question in order to 'put him to the test'.[1] Jesus had invited that man to answer his own question and the words he used were substantially the same as Jesus' answer on this occasion. Luke was recording an incident from earlier in Jesus' ministry, and the question on that occasion was not 'Which commandment is the most important of all?' but 'What shall I do to inherit eternal life?' However, the similarities between the two conversations were probably enough for Luke to decide not to include this particular meeting during Jesus' final week of ministry. It is evident from all this that the rabbis of Jesus' day were much exercised to find summary statements of the Old Testament law. Jesus had given this subject due consideration before now. If the Pharisees of Jerusalem had been aware of this background, they might have chosen their test question differently.

Jesus' answer to this question of importance

Jesus replied in terms of two great commandments about love for God with our whole being and love for our neighbour as ourselves. The words are well known to those familiar with some forms of Church of England Holy Communion services and they are drawn from two Old Testament passages (Deut. 6:4–5; Lev. 19:18).

As an aside, we need to acknowledge that this is a high standard and also, in order to avoid misunderstanding, that these two great commandments (or indeed the Ten Commandments) were never intended to be a way into heaven. God called a people to himself by redeeming them from slavery in Egypt.[2] This was his work of sovereign grace. These Old Testament commandments are instructions to those who are addressed as already being God's people. The position is the same for those of us living today in the light of the New Testament. God calls us to be his people by grace on the basis of the death of Jesus on the cross, and his commands to us in the Bible are how we are to live as those who belong to him.

'Not far from the kingdom of God'

In Matthew's short account of the incident, no response is recorded from either the lawyer or the Pharisees whom he represented. The impression is given that no answer can be given, because Jesus has said all that needs to be said on the subject.[3] But Mark provides the lawyer's obvious approval of what Jesus has said. The tone of his reply appears to be warm and respectful. He even adds extra weight to Jesus' words by quoting Hosea's statement about steadfast love being more important than sacrifice and knowledge of God being more important than burnt offerings (Hosea 6:6). No amount of religion can make up for the sin of not loving God or not loving others. This is not the reply of a critic or an opponent, and Mark tells us that Jesus saw that he answered wisely. This man was acknowledging that God's standard for his people is impossible and that religion is unable to save us. Rather, the only thing that anyone can do who acknowledges what this man did is to go on to say, in effect, 'I cannot save myself. I throw myself on your mercy. Forgive me, a helpless sinner' (cf. Luke 18:13–14).

Jesus spoke these words to the man: 'You are not far from the kingdom of God.' This is sometimes taken to be some form of rebuke, as if to tell him that, contrary to what he might be assuming, his religious observance did not qualify him for heaven ('not far from' being vastly different from 'in' or 'already belonging to'). But this lawyer already knew that, and therefore it is preferable to take these words as being a tremendous encouragement to an individual who showed commendable spiritual insight. This lawyer was standing there and then right in front of the Man who is God, the very one whom we must love wholly, also the one who alone could forgive him.

As much as we would love to know, we are simply not told what happened to this man afterwards. But what Mark does tell us is his statement of what Luke has already included, namely that following this no one dared to ask Jesus any more questions (Luke 20:40).

Prayer

Lord Jesus Christ,

You are THE TEACHER, *who alone can reveal the truths of Scripture to our finite minds and deceitful hearts.*

We thank you for the clarity of your words and your willingness to teach those who come to you in humility, and by your Spirit to give the light of the knowledge of the glory of God in your face.

We ask that we may love you, the Son, together with the Father and the Holy Spirit, with all our heart and with all our soul and with all our mind and with all our strength, and that we may love our neighbour as ourselves. Amen.

NOTES

1 Luke 10:25–28. This was the meeting that led on to Jesus telling the Parable of the Good Samaritan: Luke 10:30–37.

2 When reading the Ten Commandments in Exod. 20:3–17, it is important to notice that they follow on from God's statement of his gracious redemption of his people in Exod. 20:2.

3 This is an implicit anticipation of what will be made explicit in Matt. 22:46.

Chapter 7

Challenge 5: Jesus asks a question

(MATTHEW 22:41–46; MARK 12:35–37; LUKE 20:41–44)

Jesus on the offensive

Each of the Synoptic Gospel writers records one final round of the contest between Jesus and his critics, but this time it was Jesus who asked the question. They had previously questioned *his* authority. Now he questioned *their* authority, even their competence, to teach. 'How can they say . . . ?'—in Mark's and Luke's introductions to this little section—was a direct challenge to them.

We can imagine some interaction in the exchange between Jesus and his opponents (the Pharisees, according to Matthew, on this occasion). The question concerned the identity of the Christ. Of course, the Old Testament said that Christ would be David's descendant (2 Sam. 7:12–13), but that was not the issue. The issue was that the scribes were apparently saying that the Christ would be *no more than* a descendant of David. They regarded him as a mere man, who would have to look up to David, his great ancestor.

But Jesus quoted from Psalm 110 to show that they were wrong (110:1). David, inspired by the Holy Spirit, had called the Messiah 'my Lord'. This individual who was victorious over his enemies was enthroned with God himself.

In effect, Jesus was giving an answer to his opponents' very first question to him, in the first round of the contest—namely their question about his authority. That answer, or indeed a claim, was in effect: 'I am the Christ, the son of David (human), but I am also the Son of God (divine), and that is my authority for the things I do.'

Mark reports that 'the great throng heard him gladly'. This shows that the so-called 'authorities' had very little actual authority in the crowd's eyes. Matthew chooses this moment to include the formula, already used by Luke and Mark, about Jesus' enemies no longer daring to ask him any further questions. So, following five rounds of sparring between Jesus and the religious leaders, Israel's leaders are shown to be standing condemned and powerless. Jesus has defeated the opposition each and every time. Jesus would still face the cross at the end of the week, but it would be because he chose to do so, and not because they had forced his hand.

Prayer

Lord Jesus Christ,

You are THE SON OF DAVID and THE LORD OF DAVID.

We thank you that you are fully God and fully man and are therefore the perfect mediator between God and men—the one who gave himself as a ransom for all.

We ask that you would help us to stand in awe of your divine majesty and to rejoice in your willingness to be known as the Friend of sinners. Amen.

Judgment on hypocrites

(MATTHEW 23:1–39; MARK 12:38–40; LUKE 20:45–47)

Jesus the Judge

Following the rounds of debate between Jesus and his opponents—and particularly in the wake of their failure, following his last words to them, to recognize him as their Messiah—Jesus delivered a blistering attack on the religious hierarchy of his day. But he did so in the hearing of his disciples and the crowds, who had already been listening in to the preceding discussions. He was teaching the disciples and the crowds at the same time as he was exposing the errors of the nation's spiritual teachers, and therefore we find Jesus specifically addressing one group in some parts of his speech and another group in other parts. Jesus had criticized the Pharisees and Sadducees on earlier occasions, of course (e.g. Matt. 15:7–9 [Mark 7:5–8]; Matt. 16:5–12 [Mark 8:14–15]), but this is a very public censure, delivered in the temple precincts.

For whatever reason, Mark and Luke have chosen to give a very brief account of Jesus' condemnation of the scribes (i.e. the teachers of the law). Matthew's account is significantly longer and therefore the focus in this chapter will be on his version.

Luke includes an account of Jesus pronouncing woes on the Pharisees and teachers of the law at an earlier point in his ministry,[1] and some of the wording on that occasion is very similar to what we find here in Matthew chapter 23.

There is no denying the strong language that Jesus used in his criticism of the nation's spiritual leaders. For example, he called them 'hypocrites', 'blind guides' and 'fools', and he told them that they were 'sentenced to hell'. But Jesus was not indulging in a personal vendetta: he was delivering a judicial pronouncement. So there is no contradiction, as some have claimed, between, on the one hand, Jesus' teaching in the Sermon on the Mount about avoiding anger and pursuing love (Matt. 5:21–22, 43–48) and, on the other hand, his outspoken condemnation of the scribes and Pharisees in this chapter of Matthew's Gospel. In the former, Jesus was teaching about normal relationships between Christian people and others. In the latter, Jesus was speaking as the divine Judge, to whom all must give account. It should be noted that, even in the Sermon on the Mount, Jesus claims the right to act as Judge and to make decisions about people's eternal destiny (Matt. 7:21–23). No doubt some Jewish leaders were sympathetic to Jesus.[2] Jesus' words of condemnation here were addressed to the scribes and Pharisees in general, not to every member of that group without exception.

Matthew chapter 23 presents us with a catalogue of the symptoms of hearts that have become hardened towards God. The frightening thing is that these people were supposed to be the nation's spiritual leaders, who should by definition be models of those living in a right relationship with God. This chapter, therefore, stands as a warning to all in any generation for whom 'religion' has become more important than 'relationship'.

The scribes and Pharisees are false teachers; Jesus is the true Teacher (Matt. 23:1–12)

The theme of the opening paragraph of Jesus' attack on the religious leaders is the contrast between himself, the *true* Teacher, and them, the *false* teachers. Jesus said that they 'sit on Moses' seat' (that means that they claimed to be the successors of Moses), but in fact the 'one instructor' to whom they should have been looking was himself, 'the Christ'. It may seem strange that Jesus told the crowds and his disciples to 'practise and observe whatever they [the scribes and Pharisees] tell you', but this is best understood as a statement of biting irony. A paraphrase of the opening part of Jesus' words might be as follows: 'The scribes and Pharisees *claim* to be authoritative teachers wearing the mantle of Moses. If that were indeed the case, you must of course obey them. But, in fact, you should *not* follow their teaching. The *reality*—in contrast to their claim—is that they place legalistic burdens on you without offering you any help at all. They do more harm than good.' The 'heavy burdens' that they imposed contrast with the 'rest' that Jesus earlier promised to those who would come to him, with the assurance that the 'yoke' of his authority is easy (Matt. 11:28–30).

Jesus went on to give examples of their wrong practices. He referred to their ostentatious show of piety and their love of receiving honour and applause. He attacked their love of titles, whether it be 'rabbi', 'father' or 'instructor'. Instead, people should recognize God alone as Father and himself (the Christ) as their only teacher and instructor. Jesus was making here an amazing claim to be divine by placing his role as the one true teacher (the Christ) immediately before and after the role of God as Father. Jesus went on to conclude his opening comments with a statement of the two key qualities that should characterize members of God's kingdom—namely *service* and *humility*. As Jesus had taught on an earlier occasion, he himself is the model of both of these qualities. Power-seeking authority was not to be a mark of Christ's disciples, he had said. Rather, 'whoever would be great among you must be your servant, and whoever would be first among you must be your slave, even as the Son of Man came not to be served but to serve, and to give his life as a ransom for many' (Matt. 20:26–28 [Mark 10:43–45]).

Seven woes (Matt. 23:13–32)

The major part of the rest of the chapter consists of a series of seven 'woes' that Jesus pronounced on the scribes and Pharisees. These woes are primarily expressions of condemnation, spoken by the Judge, but the word 'woe' also suggests a note of compassion, which anticipates the final paragraph of the chapter.[3]

There is a recognizable pattern in the seven woes. They form what is known technically as a 'chiasmus', which means that the ideas are placed symmetrically: the first and the last mirror each other; so too do the second and the second to last; and so on, working inwards from both ends, with the central item being given a particular emphasis. There are at least three things that can make a chiasmus effective. First, by being structured and ordered it can give a picture of the totality of the argument. Second, the important key point at the centre is clearly identified. Third, particular emphasis is also given to the very first and the very last items. All three of these effects apply to the chiasmus of these verses.

It will be most helpful to work our way towards the centre of this section from the beginning and the end in conjunction with each other. In so doing, it will be simpler to identify the matching themes.

The *first and seventh woes* can be labelled: *You fail to recognize Jesus as the Messiah* (1st woe, v. 13) *just as those before you failed to recognize the prophets* (7th woe, vv. 29–32).[4]

- Jesus began by stating the way in which the scribes and Pharisees caused most spiritual damage to those whom they influenced. By failing to recognize Jesus as the Christ, as they had done repeatedly (not least in the preceding series of five encounters), they had done their utmost to prevent people from coming to Jesus, who is the one and only entry point to the kingdom of heaven (John 14:6). Jesus called them 'hypocrites' because they claimed to be teaching God's law, but in fact they taught error. *(Woe 1)*
- Their hypocrisy was evident too in their professed admiration of the Old Testament prophets, when in fact they were no different from their spiritual forebears who rejected, and even killed, the prophets.[5] *(Woe 7)*

The *second and sixth woes* may be summed up as: *You appear to be busy for God, but you are causing serious spiritual damage* (v. 15 and vv. 27–28).

- The scribes and Pharisees were keen on missionary work and went to great lengths to make disciples. But their 'converts' were drawn not to a living relationship with God, but to an even more extreme form of bigoted Pharisaism than theirs. *(Woe 2)*

- They followed the custom of regularly whitewashing grave sites in order to warn pilgrims to avoid ritual uncleanness by contact with dead bodies. But this was an apt picture of their hypocrisy, because in reality they themselves were far more dangerous than poorly identified graves: their influence contaminated those who followed them. *(Woe 6)*

The *third and fifth woes* can be given the title: *You misuse Scripture* (vv. 16–22 and vv. 25–26).

- The scribes and Pharisees taught that there were different kinds of oaths that a person might swear, some of which were binding and some of which were not. They may have done this as an attempt to correct widespread abuse of oaths. But the result of the complicated distinctions that they taught was to make it easier for people to make promises which they had no intention of keeping. In effect, they were promoting lying. Jesus always insisted that Scripture teaches people to tell the truth (Matt. 5:33–37). *(Woe 3)*
- The Pharisees had their own man-made traditions about the need for ritual cleansing. On an earlier occasion, Jesus criticized their insistence on the ceremonial washing of hands (Matt. 15:1–3 [Mark 7:1–8]; Luke 11:39ff.). Here, Jesus criticized them for their rules about the ceremonial washing of crockery. Their mistake was to elevate their own teachings about *external* cleansing and to ignore the plain teaching of Scripture that what is needed is *internal* cleansing of the heart (Matt. 15:10–20 [Mark 7:14–23]; Ps. 51; Jer. 17:9). *(Woe 5)*

The *fourth woe*—the central one—follows on from the above-mentioned pair: *You do not understand what Scripture is all about!* (vv. 23–24).

- The scribes and Pharisees were concerned with peripheral matters of the law and, as a result, had 'neglected the weightier matters of the law', which Jesus identified as justice, mercy and faithfulness. If they had truly known the Scriptures, they would have had a better sense of proportion (e.g. Ps. 33:5; Micah 6:8; Zech. 7:9). According to Jesus, their failure to have a right perspective on Scripture was on a par with 'straining out a gnat and swallowing a camel'. Both of these were regarded as unclean. *(Woe 4)*

Jesus concludes his indictment (Matt. 23:33–36)

Undoubtedly, Jesus was building up to a conclusion in his condemnation of the scribes and Pharisees. The assumption being made here is that the closing comments begin at verse 33 of Matthew 23, where Jesus addressed the religious leaders as 'serpents' and 'vipers'. But some of the content of the conclusion flows out of the content of the seventh woe. In particular, Jesus continued the theme of their similarity to earlier generations who rejected and murdered the prophets. With heavy irony, Jesus urged them to 'Fill up . . . the measure of [their] fathers.' The inclusion of the word 'crucify' as one of the actions of which they would be guilty must be seen as Jesus confronting these religious leaders with the enormity of what they were intending to do to him within a short space of time.

The specific mention of the murdered Abel and Zechariah (Gen. 4:8; 2 Chr. 24:20–21) reflects the structure of the Hebrew Old Testament Scriptures, which consisted of three parts (the Law, the Prophets and the Writings), with Chronicles being the last book in the Writings. So these two individuals were literally the first and the last godly people whose murders are recorded in the Hebrew Scriptures.[6]

Frighteningly, in the last verse of Jesus' speech, he included not only the teachers of the law and the Pharisees but also 'this generation' as those who faced condemnation. The sins of the leaders made the people guilty, because they (the people) had sided with their leaders. They had not heeded Jesus' warnings. They had not transferred their allegiance to Jesus, whom they should have recognized as their true Christ and King.

Jesus did not at this stage specify what 'these things' would be that would come upon them. He would elaborate on that in the following chapter of Matthew's Gospel (and the parallel passages). However, it was evident from what was included here that it would be the punishment for blood-guilt, and that is a serious matter.

As we look back over the whole of Matthew 23 up to this point, we can take in more fully the key points that arise from this analysis of Jesus' critique of the scribes and Pharisees. It will be evident that the *source* of their error was a failure to understand the essence of Scripture (woe 4—the central woe). The *end result* of their error was their failure to recognize Jesus as the Christ (woes 1 and 7—the first and the last of the series). Their catalogue of errors embraced the misuse of Scripture and spiritual damage inflicted on others.

Rarely has a judge delivered a more devastating indictment on the accused than this Judge. But it would be short-sighted of us today to take this section of Scripture as an encouragement to gloat over Jesus' condemnation of the faults of those with whom we disagree. We would do far better to examine ourselves, because it is all too easy for professing believers of any generation to mistake the appearance of godliness for its reality and power and to substitute religious activity for a close walk with God.

Jesus' lament over Jerusalem (Matt. 23:37–39)

Jesus' lament over Jerusalem follows on immediately from his severe condemnation of the nation's spiritual leaders. The juxtaposition is altogether amazing. But we have already noticed Jesus' compassion for the people when the context has been one of judgment, as when he entered the capital and cleansed the temple.[7]

Jesus' compassion was intense, as evidenced by his double naming of

'Jerusalem' as the city he addressed.[8] Jesus was not blind to the nation's glaring sins, referring yet again to their murders of prophets. He went on to paint two moving word pictures. The first was of himself as a hen with maternal love for her chicks, who—contrary to nature—perversely refuse to come under her wings for protection.[9] The second was of the nation as a desolate house, as if devastated by enemy attack. The implication is that the 'house' of the nation has been abandoned by its owner, who is God—or Jesus. Given that Jesus is 'Immanuel (which means, God with us)' (Matt. 1:23), this is a serious matter.

What did Jesus mean by his final words of the chapter, 'For I tell you, you will not see me again, until you say, "Blessed is he who comes in the name of the Lord"'? The crowd had shouted those words on Palm Sunday when Jesus entered Jerusalem.[10] The answer can only be that Jesus was referring to his Second Coming, as, following his ministry in Jerusalem during these few days, he would make no further public appearances before his people until his return at the end of time. While he was being rejected now, the time will come when his people will welcome him and acclaim him—and will do so in a far more perfect way than the people of Jerusalem had done a short time earlier at his Triumphal Entry. So this very last verse of Matthew chapter 23 prepares the way for the dominant theme of the Second Coming in Matthew chapter 24 (and the parallel passages in Mark and Luke) and in Matthew chapter 25. Jesus' Second Coming will be a time of judgment *and* celebration.

Prayer

Lord Jesus Christ,

We acknowledge again that you are THE JUDGE. *You expose the hypocrisy of all who have the appearance of godliness but deny its power, who claim to be lovers of God but are in reality lovers of self.*

We ask that we may rightly handle the word of truth and in everything may adorn the doctrine of God our Saviour.

Chapter 8

Would you teach us the lessons of service and humility as members of the kingdom of heaven.

We thank you that, even while you speak as Judge, you have compassion for those who are like sheep without a shepherd, and you long for them to come to you. Amen.

NOTES

1   Luke 11:39–52. Luke places this incident in the context of a meal in a Pharisee's house, when Jesus responded to the Pharisee's astonishment that Jesus did not participate in ceremonial washing before the meal.

2   For example, Joseph of Arimathea and Nicodemus: John 19:38–40.

3   'Woes' formed part of the message of some of the Old Testament prophets, e.g. Isaiah, Jeremiah, Ezekiel, Habakkuk and Zephaniah.

4   Matt. 23:14 is omitted in modern Bible versions because it does not appear in the earliest and most reliable manuscripts. Where it does appear, as in the Authorized Version, the wording is the same as Mark 12:40 (Luke 20:47) and has been inserted from there.

5   This was, of course, referred to in Matthew's and Mark's versions of the Parable of the Tenants (Matt. 21:35–36; Mark 12:4–5).

6   The fact that Abel and Zechariah may appear to be the first and the last of an alphabetical list of Old Testament martyrs (a literal 'A to Z') is purely coincidental. The Zechariah of 2 Chr. 24:20–21 is described as 'the son of Jehoiada', whereas in Matt. 23:35 he is called 'the son of Barachiah'. One of the possible solutions for this apparent discrepancy is that Jehoiada—a significant individual in 2 Chr. 22–24—may have been Zechariah's grandfather (not father), as Jehoiada's death at the age of 130 is recorded before the account of Zechariah's ministry and murder. It is not unusual in the Old Testament for 'son' to be used in this way—just as the later prophet Zechariah was known both as 'the son of Berechiah' (Zech. 1:1) and as 'the son of Iddo' (Ezra 6:14), but Zech. 1:1 identifies the prophet as Iddo's grandson. If this is correct, it is possible that Barachiah (Matt. 23:35) was the son of Jehoiada and the father of Zechariah. Another possible solution is that 'the son of Barachiah' in Matt. 23:35 is a textual

addition by a scribe who thought that the Zechariah being referred to was the later prophet just mentioned. (The spellings of names in this note are those found in the ESV.)

7 Particularly Luke 19:41–44. See also the discussion in the Introduction on Luke 13:34–35; 19:41–44; Matt. 23:37–39.

8 Instances of double naming of those addressed, for intensified emotional impact, can be found in the Old Testament. A particularly striking example is David's lament for Absalom (2 Sam. 18:33).

9 Jesus was undoubtedly echoing Ruth 2:12 at this point: Ruth, a foreigner, had come to take refuge under the wings of the LORD, the God of Israel—but God's own people despised those wings of refuge. In the same way, Isa. 1:2–3 records God's words about the unnatural rebellion of his people against his fatherly love, in contrast to members of the animal kingdom.

10 Matt. 21:9. The quotation is from Ps. 118:26.

Chapter 9

An example to follow

(MARK 12:41–44; LUKE 21:1–4)

The widow's offering

This short section concerning the widow's offering appears only in Mark's and Luke's Gospels. These two writers present her as a direct contrast to the scribes, against whom Jesus has been warning in the previous few verses of their accounts (their abridged versions of the lengthy denunciation of the religious hierarchy found in Matthew's Gospel). One of the crimes of these spiritual leaders was to 'devour widows' houses'. Very fittingly, therefore, we are told that Jesus singled out one poor widow as an example to follow.

This woman gave to God's treasury all that she owned, little as that was. In today's equivalent money that would be worth less than £1. She trusted God and expressed her total dependence on him in concrete terms. She was so different from the wealthy, who gave only some of their plenty. It is implied, by the juxtaposition of this short paragraph and the preceding one, that these wealthy people included the scribes. It is implied also that the wealthy went about their giving ostentatiously, seeking the admiration of others. No one, except Jesus, had eyes for the poor widow as she made her offering.

This paragraph not only provides teaching about giving and about genuine, humble and trusting devotion to God. It also contains a lesson about salvation. Neither two small coins nor a much larger sum of money can buy salvation. We owe our whole life to him who himself has bought salvation for us. Whether or not this woman would be able to express her faith in these terms, she looked to God as much as any of the Old Testament Israelites who, like the people of Hebrews chapter 11, are 'commended through their faith' (Heb. 11:39–40). This woman's devotion and her giving represented the overflow of a heart that was in tune with God. And it is supremely in this respect that Jesus singled her out as an example for us to follow.

Prayer

Lord Jesus Christ,

You are THE GUARDIAN of the humble and lowly.

We thank you that you never lose sight of those who, in their need, look to you.

We ask you to help us not to seek the praise of the world, but to make it our aim to please you. Amen.

Be prepared!

(MATTHEW 24:1–51; MARK 13:1–37; LUKE 21:5–38)

An overview

This section of the Gospel narrative has generated a considerable amount of discussion, far more than many other passages in the Bible, resulting in widely divergent views being put forward. To say that some disagreement surrounds this section would be to put the matter mildly. No attempt will be made here to engage with that ongoing debate; instead we will unpack what appears to be the plain meaning of these passages in Matthew, Mark and Luke. There are, of course, variations between the three Synoptic writers—less so between Matthew and Mark, and more so between Luke and the other two writers—but none of those differences poses any major difficulty in making sense of the texts or prevents us from recognizing that all three writers are in full agreement. In fact, placing the three accounts alongside each other helps to clarify the meaning of the text. Luke's account is somewhat shorter and, understandably—as he was writing mainly for the benefit of a Gentile audience—he leaves out some details included by Mark which would have been more significant for Jewish readers, such as the mention of the Mount of Olives or 'the abomination of desolation'.[1]

As we shall see in more detail, Jesus' teaching here covers the whole of the history of the world from Jesus' crucifixion (together with his resurrection and ascension) to 'the end' (or 'the end of the age'), as Jesus expresses it. But there are two particular periods within the whole sweep of human history to which Jesus gives particular attention. One is the fall of Jerusalem in AD 70, when the Romans utterly destroyed the city, including the temple. The other is 'the end' itself, the time of Christ's Second Coming (or 'the coming of the Son of Man').

These two events—the fall of Jerusalem and Christ's Second Coming—

are related. The judgment that fell on Jerusalem within forty years of Jesus' teaching here has to be understood as a curtain-raiser (an anticipation on a small scale) of the judgment to fall on the world when Christ comes again. An understanding of this connection between the two events should prevent us from regarding the horrific end of the Jewish War as merely an unfortunate incident of ancient history. But there is a further point that we should recognize. Jesus made a prediction about what would happen to Jerusalem four decades ahead of the fulfilment of that prediction—and there can be no doubt that Jesus was absolutely correct in his prediction. The challenge, therefore, for us today (as in any other generation in the Christian era) is to trust Jesus in what he has predicted concerning the future of the world and his return at the end of time. He has not returned yet, but one day he will.

It will be helpful to give an overview of this section of the Gospel narrative, in order to help us navigate our way through the subsequent study—and this understanding is reflected in the way the Gospel texts are arranged in the Appendix.

	Matthew	Mark	Luke
Jesus' foretelling of the destruction of the temple—and the disciples' questions	24:1–3	13:1–4	21:5–7
A road map to the end (A)	24:4–14	13:5–13	21:8–19
The fall of Jerusalem	24:15–21	13:14–19	21:20–24
A road map to the end (B)	24:22–28	13:20–23	-
The coming of the Son of Man	24:29–31	13:24–27	21:25–28
Reading the signs of the times	24:32–35	13:28–31	21:29–33
Being prepared for the end	24:36–51	13:32–37	21:34–36

Jesus' foretelling of the destruction of the temple—and the disciples' questions (Matt. 24:1–3; Mark 13:1–4; Luke 21:5–7)

There may well be some symbolic significance in Jesus' departure from the temple, leaving the city and going to the Mount of Olives opposite the temple, to which Matthew and Mark (but not Luke) draw attention. In the book of Ezekiel, the prophet had a vision of the glory of God leaving the temple and coming to rest on the Mount of Olives.[2] That was in the context of God's judgment on Jerusalem and his people at the time of the Babylonian exile, prior to the Babylonians moving in and destroying the city, including Solomon's temple. We have seen in the preceding chapters of the Gospels that Jesus had already sounded a note of judgment on the temple. In the incident of the fig tree, Jesus in effect passed sentence, and therefore—just as with the fig tree—after a delay judgment would fall. Now Jesus was about to pronounce with unmistakable clarity the destruction of the city by the Romans. In the light of all this, Jesus' change of location from the temple area to the Mount of Olives, to the east, must be seen as a deliberate echo of Ezekiel's vision. It follows from this, of course, that Jesus was claiming to be none other than God in his glory.

Zechariah, too, refers to the Mount of Olives in his apocalyptic vision of the coming day of the Lord (Zech. 14:4). It is possible that Jesus also had this in mind when he chose to give his teaching about his Second Coming from that place.

While still in the temple area, the disciples seem to have forgotten all that Jesus had been saying in the preceding period of time about God's judgment to come on the temple and the city. Instead, they began to behave like enthusiastic tourists, impressed by the architectural splendour of the temple, which had been greatly embellished in recent time by Herod the Great. Jesus had to spell out to them that the temple would become a scene of utter devastation and ruin.

Jesus' reply led to the disciples asking him for further clarification. It would seem that Peter, James, John and Andrew were the main spokesmen, with the rest of the disciples listening in. We can imagine that the disciples asked a number of questions, and each of the Gospel writers gives his edited version of those questions. It is likely that the disciples understood the destruction of Jerusalem and Jesus' Second Coming as a single event, and it is Matthew's version that spells out most precisely what they had in mind: 'Tell us, when will these things be, and what will be the sign of your coming and of the close of the age?' Matthew uses the word 'coming' (*parousia* is the word in Greek) to refer to what we normally term Jesus' Second Coming. The word was commonly used of the coming of a king or ruler. Four of the twenty-four occurrences of the word in the New Testament are to be found in Matthew chapter 24.

A road map to the end (A) (Matt. 24:4–14; Mark 13:5–13; Luke 21:8–19)

In all three Gospels, the first part of Jesus' reply to the disciples covers the whole of human history from that point on until 'the end'. That is the term that Matthew uses in Matthew 24:13 and 14, and Mark in Mark 13:13. Luke does not use that expression, but his version of this part of Jesus' teaching runs in parallel to Matthew and Mark and likewise is meant to cover the whole period until Christ's return. Jesus has in mind a long period of time. While the signs that he refers to will be evident in the experience of people of that generation, he warns, 'but the end is not yet'. In fact, he says, 'these are but the beginning of the birth pains'. 'You' (Matt. 24:9; Mark 13:9) includes all Christian believers, not only those of that time. Jesus' concern was not to give an academic answer to the disciples' questions but to be thoroughly practical for their benefit and the benefit of every subsequent generation of believers. His teaching is certainly not about sign-spotting or date-setting. The word 'then' in Matthew 24:9 does not mean 'next', as if it is indicating a sequence; it means 'at that time'. Jesus' teaching is about waiting and not panicking; holding on when things look shaky; trusting when things seem to go wrong; keeping our Christian feet firmly on the ground; and getting on with faithful Christian living. He gives a strong encouragement to all Christian believers to endure to the end.

According to Jesus, the whole Christian era will be characterized by the following:

- False Christs (Matthew, Mark, Luke);
- Wars and rumours of wars (Matthew, Mark, Luke);
- Natural disasters, such as famines and earthquakes (Matthew, Mark, Luke)—and plagues and 'terrors and great signs from heaven' (Luke);
- Persecution of Christians (Matthew, Mark, Luke). Matthew uses the word 'tribulation' (Matt. 24:9);[3]
- Hostility towards Christian believers from family members—and even betrayal of them to the authorities (Mark and Luke);
- Apostasy by many (Matthew);
- False prophets (Matthew);
- Lawlessness (Matthew).

There can be no denying that every one of these terrifying and unsettling phenomena has been evident throughout the past two millennia.

But alongside the warnings of the dangers that lie ahead, Jesus' teaching also includes some great encouragements:

- Opportunities for evangelism (Matthew, Mark, Luke). Both Matthew and Mark include words about the gospel (or 'the gospel of the kingdom') being proclaimed throughout the whole world. The book of Acts gives an account of the gospel being preached throughout the whole Roman world—in Jesus' words, 'in Jerusalem and in all Judea and Samaria, and to the end of the earth' (Acts 1:8). In the centuries since then, and particularly in the last three hundred years, Christian missionary work has reached many of the remotest parts of the world. Mark and Luke refer to Christians bearing witness to kings and governors.[4]
- Mark and Luke add in the assurance that Christian believers in

such situations will be given words and wisdom in those times when they are hauled up before the authorities on account of their Christian faith.

- Luke includes the assurance 'But not a hair of your head will perish.' Given that this promise comes immediately after the warning that some believers will be put to death, the assurance has to do with the perspective of eternity, as in Jesus' promise 'I give them eternal life, and they will never perish, and no one will snatch them out of my hand' (John 10:28).

The fall of Jerusalem (Matt. 24:15–21; Mark 13:14–19; Luke 21:20–24)

Each of the three Synoptic Gospel writers records Jesus moving on to a section of teaching about the fall of Jerusalem. Having dealt with the whole panorama of world history from his First Coming to his Second Coming and all the suffering (or 'tribulation') that will be experienced throughout all that time, Jesus turns his focus now specifically on to one episode of 'tribulation' which would occur within a relatively short space of time. The reason for this has already been explained, but it is important to recognize that Jesus *does* switch the focus for the next few verses of each Gospel.

In Matthew and Mark, Jesus begins by referring to 'the abomination of desolation'. In Matthew we are told that this is a reference to the book of Daniel, whereas in Mark it is left to readers to make the connection themselves. 'Let the reader understand' (in both Matthew and Mark) is best understood as Jesus' own comment, pointing to the book of Daniel, rather than as an additional comment by the Gospel writers. In Daniel, this phrase referred to an act of desecration in the temple which would be carried out by the Seleucid king Antiochus IV Epiphanes in 168 BC.[5] He devoted himself to the destruction of everything that the Jewish religion stood for, forbidding sacrifices and abolishing religious festivals and Sabbath observance. The climax came when he placed an armed guard in the temple area and desecrated the sanctuary itself by erecting an altar to Zeus and sacrificing a pig on it. Jesus uses the language of that event to say that the same kind of thing will happen again. He is pointing ahead to the desecration of the temple by the Romans in AD 70, which was carried out even more thoroughly than the earlier outrage, as this time the temple was razed to the ground. Luke, who—as we have seen—was writing for a Gentile audience, does not refer specifically to the temple but focuses on Jerusalem being surrounded by armies, which would lead to its 'desolation'.

Jesus gives instructions that, as soon as this scenario begins to unfold, people should make an immediate departure from the city. Historically, Christians did abandon Jerusalem halfway through the siege. With characteristic compassion, Jesus expresses pity for expectant mothers and those with very young children caught up in this perilous situation. The historian Josephus recorded the horrific nature of the Romans' devastation of Jerusalem, bearing out Jesus' comment about the unparalleled 'tribulation' of those days. There have been many other terrible atrocities in the course of human history, and the millions killed under Hitler, Stalin, Pol Pot and others in the last century come to mind. But the degree, if not the extent, of the suffering at the fall of Jerusalem was unique. The percentage of Jerusalem's population who were completely and cruelly exterminated or enslaved was beyond compare.

Luke, more clearly than Matthew or Mark, leaves us in no doubt that the destruction of Jerusalem would be an act of judgment from God. He includes Jesus' words 'for these are days of vengeance, to fulfil all that is written'. The latter part of this statement points to God's warnings in the Old Testament that disobedience to him would result in retribution. And now the nation was about to turn its back on God's own Son. But Jesus' words in Luke also carry a note of hope: the devastation of Jerusalem would be 'until the times of the Gentiles are fulfilled'. The cross would lead not only to the rejection of Israel but to a long period of opportunity for the Gentiles to hear and welcome the good news of the gospel (see Rom. 11:25). Jesus had taught only a short time earlier that Israel's failure to welcome him would be followed by the extension of the gospel invitation to the Gentiles (Matt. 21:43 [Mark 12:9; Luke 20:16]; Matt. 22:8–9).

A road map to the end (B) (Matt. 24:22–28; Mark 13:20–23)

Luke's account, unlike Matthew's and Mark's, omits any further teaching by Jesus on the subject of 'the road map to the end'. Instead, he moves straight on to Jesus' words about his Second Coming, which Matthew and Mark come to in a few verses' time.

But Matthew and Mark both show Jesus returning at this point to teaching about the whole period of history from his First Coming to his Second Coming. The clue that this is what Jesus is doing is his repetition of his earlier warnings about false christs and false prophets. The one new element included here is that impostors may try to persuade people by performing signs and wonders: supernatural powers are not in themselves evidence of genuineness. The earlier and later warnings about false christs serve as bookends for the whole section, which began in Matthew 24:4 and Mark 13:4. The technical term for this device is an 'inclusio'. The *specific* teaching about the fall of Jerusalem is sandwiched between two sections of *general* teaching about the whole period of time until 'the end'. Mark's account provides an additional link between the two parts of the 'road map to the end' by recording Jesus' words 'be on your guard' in each (Mark 13:9 and 23).

This means that 'those days' (Matthew), or just 'the days' (Mark), which God has mercifully cut short 'for the sake of the elect [i.e. true believers]', refer to the sufferings experienced by Christians all down the ages. Without this assurance of that period of time being shortened, the cumulative effect of the natural disasters, persecution, wars, and so on, that Jesus has listed a little earlier could cause believers to despair.

In Matthew, Jesus draws a contrast between the *secret* claims of the impostors, calling people to the 'wilderness' or to 'inner rooms', with the *public* nature—when it happens—of Christ's Second Coming. The 'coming of the Son of Man' will be seen by absolutely everybody in the world, just as lightning lights up the whole sky: nobody will fail to notice Jesus' return. The proverb that Jesus quotes about the corpse and the vultures almost certainly reinforces the same point. It will be as impossible for humanity to fail to see the coming of the Son of Man as it is for vultures to miss carrion. Jesus' choice of this proverb deliberately conveys an ominous hint of death and destruction for those who are unprepared.

The coming of the Son of Man (Matt. 24:29–31; Mark 13:24–27; Luke 21:25–28)
The next few verses in each of the three Gospels record Jesus' focused teaching on his Second Coming at the end of time. Jesus' phrase recorded in Matthew, 'immediately after the tribulation of those days', refers to the whole Christian era, not to the fall of Jerusalem. The same applies to the version reported in Mark: 'in those days, after that tribulation'.

All three Gospel writers tell us that Jesus' Second Coming will be accompanied by astronomical phenomena. It is difficult to say if they are to be understood as literal or metaphorical. The answer is probably both. The end of the world cannot be envisaged as anything other than an event of cosmic proportions. Luke records Jesus' words about the 'distress', 'perplexity', 'fear' and 'foreboding' experienced by people on earth at that time.

Jesus' description of the coming of the Son of Man uses the language of one of Daniel's visions, which Jesus will refer to again at his trial before the Sanhedrin (Dan. 7:13–14; Matt. 26:64; Mark 14:62; Luke 22:69). The phrase '*the sign* of the Son of Man' in Matthew is probably best understood as an ensign, or standard, in a military sense, which fits in well with the 'trumpet call' of the following verse. On this understanding, the return of Christ will be a triumphant declaration of victory.

However, Matthew's version also tells us, with an echo of Zechariah (Zech. 12:10–12), that 'all the tribes of the earth will mourn'. This would suggest a belated recognition by unbelievers of who it is they have failed to acknowledge and worship—and of the terrible truth that the door of opportunity to repent and believe, which during their lifetimes had been open to them, is now closed for ever.

For Christian believers, Christ's Second Coming is good news. They are 'the elect' whom the angels will gather to him from the four corners of the earth (as we might express it). There is no place in the universe where any of Jesus' followers might be forgotten or overlooked. Luke adds Jesus' encouragement to believers: 'straighten up and raise your heads, because your redemption is drawing near'. While it is true that those who have put their trust in Jesus are already redeemed, the fulfilment, or consummation, of that redemption waits until we are with Christ in heaven.

Reading the signs of the times (Matt. 24:32–35; Mark 13:28–31; Luke 21:29–33)
All three Gospel writers record Jesus bringing the disciples' attention back to the general flow of the history of mankind, which will lead up to the Second Coming. This is the most satisfactory way to understand the next few verses, rather than to see the focus continuing to be specifically on the Second Coming. Here is teaching about the mindset of Christian believers in the here and now as they read the signs of the times and prepare for all that lies ahead.

Jesus draws a teaching point from fig trees. This, of course, brings to mind the earlier incident of the cursing of the fig tree which bore no fruit—a symbol of a nation that bore no spiritual fruit (Matt. 21:18ff.; Mark 11:12–14, 20ff.). So the mere mention of a fig tree sounds a warning of judgment. Here, however, the point is that, just as the appearance of leaves on a fig tree is a sure sign that summer is coming, in the same way 'these things'—referring to all the items that Jesus has itemized earlier in this teaching to the disciples (the tribulation and natural disasters, etc., and the fall of Jerusalem)—are a sure sign that God is working out his purposes and that will lead finally to 'the end'. Christian believers, therefore, should live in a state of readiness every day, because it is always true that 'he is near, at the very gates' (Matthew and Mark) and that 'the kingdom of God is near' (Luke).

However, there is no pinpointing of the date of Jesus' Second Coming—and Jesus will have more to say a little later about even his ignorance of that date. On the other hand, Jesus does give a straightforward indication that 'all these things' (which, as in the previous verse in each Gospel, means the beginning of all the signs of distress, including the fall of Jerusalem) will take place within a matter of years. His words about 'this generation' not passing away until all has taken place must refer to the destruction of the temple and the city.

Jesus announces with divine authority the eternal validity of his words. Just as Joshua, hundreds of years earlier, was able to say 'not one word has failed of all the good things that the LORD your God promised concerning you. All have come to pass for you; not one of them has failed' (Josh. 23:14), similarly Christians today can know for sure that, although heaven and earth will pass away, Jesus' words will not pass away. 'The word of the Lord remains for ever' (1 Peter 1:25, quoting Isa. 40:8).

Being prepared for the end (Matt. 24:36–51; Mark 13:32–37; Luke 21:34–36)
The last part of Jesus' extended reply to the disciples' questions concerns readiness for Christ's Second Coming in all three Gospels.

Matthew's and Mark's versions both begin with Jesus' statement that the timing of Jesus' return is known only to the Father. Neither the angels nor even Jesus himself, the Son, knows when that day will come. We should not be puzzled by Jesus' confession of his own ignorance on this subject, as if somehow that detracts from his divinity. It is a recurring theme throughout the New Testament that, as Paul puts it, 'though he was in the form of God, [he] did not count equality with God a thing to be grasped, but made himself nothing, taking the form of a servant, being born in the likeness of men' (Phil. 2:6–7). The word used for 'form' in each of its two occurrences in that Bible quotation ('the form of God' and 'the form of a servant') points to the real substance of his being, not an appearance. Jesus was—and is—both fully God and fully man. In his role as the Son and in his humbling of himself to go to the cross as an atoning sacrifice, he voluntarily submitted himself to the Father, so that there are times in the Gospels when we see him laying aside his divine prerogatives.

Matthew includes words from Jesus about the parallel between the coming of the Flood in the days of Noah and the coming of the Son of Man at the appointed time. Life was proceeding with quite ordinary activities in Noah's time: people 'were eating and drinking, marrying and giving in marriage'. But they were 'unaware until the flood came and swept them all away'. The implication is that at the end many will similarly be engaged in the normal affairs of life but will be totally 'unaware' and unprepared for the coming of the Son of Man.

Matthew also includes two little word pictures: one about two men working in the field, the other about two women grinding at the mill. In both these short scenes, one of the two is taken and the other is left behind. These two snapshots concerning Christ's Second Coming have led, in some circles, to the mistaken doctrine of a secret 'rapture', as if the world will be suddenly depopulated of Christians and all those left behind will realize that they have missed out on heaven. In fact, it is not stated whether the ones taken are Christians being taken to glory or non-Christians being taken to punishment. But a secret rapture cannot be the point being made here. After all, Jesus has been teaching that his coming will be public and cataclysmic. It is always dangerous to build a doctrine on a single verse (or even a couple of verses). The point about these two verses is both the unexpectedness of Christ's Second Coming and the division that his return will bring about between those who have been very close. For example, the two women in the second word picture could be a mother and daughter working together in the home. But Jesus' return will expose the fault lines between believers and unbelievers, wherever they run.

Matthew and Mark spell out Jesus' application. It is, quite simply: be prepared. In the version in Matthew, it is 'Therefore, stay awake, for you do not know on what day your Lord is coming.' Mark's version has the command 'Be on guard'—the third time in this chapter that these words have appeared (Mark 13:9, 23, 33). Luke records a more detailed command from Jesus about what is meant by being prepared. It includes avoiding wild excesses that might threaten to 'weigh down' our hearts. 'Staying awake' is to be accompanied by prayer for strength to escape all the perils of that time and to stand before the Son of Man.

Two short parables conclude Jesus' reply to his disciples in Matthew 24, spelling out what is meant by readiness and watchfulness in view of the coming day of Christ's return. In fact, these two parables can be regarded as the first two of *five* sections on this topic beginning at Matthew 24:43 and extending to the end of Matthew 25. All of these five sections, except the last, are in the form of parables.[6] Because the three passages in Matthew 25 are more substantial and better known, they will be examined separately in the next chapter of this study. But all five have to do with being prepared for the Last Day.

The first of the two short parables grabs the attention of its hearers by the somewhat surprising comparison between Jesus' return and a thief breaking into a house during the night. The point of similarity is, of course, that in neither case is it known in advance at what time the event will take place. If a house owner were to know that a break-in was due to take place, unlikely as that scenario may be, he would stay awake to prevent the intrusion. If Christian people know in advance that Jesus will return—as indeed they do, because Jesus himself has given notice—they are to 'stay awake', in the sense of living consciously in expectation of his coming, even though they do not know when that will be.

The second short parable pictures Christian people as a servant who is entrusted with the responsibility of running the master's house during his absence. The 'faithful and wise servant' is the one whom the master, on his return, finds carrying out his duties. In contrast, a servant who treats his master's absence as an excuse to act as a tyrant over his fellow servants and to feast on the master's food and drink will find, when his master returns unexpectedly, that a severe punishment awaits him. In fact, Jesus spells out the nature of that punishment in horrific terms which echo those we have already noted that he used on other occasions to warn about the reality of hell for those who resist the gospel (Matt. 8:12; 13:42, 50; 22:13; 24:51; 25:30).

Mark records one short parable in order to round off his account of Jesus' teaching on the Mount of Olives. It may be a different version of the second parable in Matthew or it may be a separate parable that Jesus told. This one concerns a servant who is given the responsibility of being the doorkeeper while his master is absent. Other servants, we are told, are given other jobs to be getting on with. But it is the doorkeeper on whom this short parable focuses. He is to 'stay awake' for his master's return. In the same way, Christians are to 'stay awake' for their Master's return.

Both the second short parable in Matthew and the parable in Mark alert us to the truth that waiting for Christ's return and 'staying awake' are not to be understood in a self-absorbed or privatized way. Christian believers are called to be actively engaged in the work of the kingdom just as the servants in the two parables were given their duties to perform during their master's absence. The work of the kingdom to which Christian believers are called while they await Christ's Second Coming is spelt out more fully in other parts of the New Testament, and it includes

Christian missionary and evangelistic activity, of which ordinary Christian witness is an essential part.[7]

Luke's ending (Luke 21:37–38)

Luke closes his account of Jesus' teaching with a comment that Jesus taught every day in the temple and that all the people came to hear him. Luke made a similar comment in Luke 19:47–48, following Jesus' cleansing of the temple and immediately before Jesus' various rounds of debate with the religious hierarchy. Those two similar statements form an 'inclusio' around the whole of Jesus' recorded teaching during these few days in Jerusalem. We met this device a little earlier: it is the equivalent of a pair of bookends holding together all the material in between.

Prayer

Lord Jesus Christ,

You are THE SON OF MAN, *who one day will come in clouds and with your power and glory to bring this world order to a close.*

We thank you for your sovereign control of human history from the beginning to the end, so that not one single detail is outside your knowledge or grasp.

We ask that we may be realists in our view of all that faces your people in the world today: both its pain and its opportunities.

Help us rightly to read the signs of the times and to know that you are not slow to fulfil your promise to come again.

By your grace, equip us to stay awake for your return. Amen.

NOTES

1 Luke includes a section of teaching delivered by Jesus on the subject of the coming of the kingdom of God, in response to questioning by Pharisees at an earlier point in his ministry, in Luke 17:20–37. Some of the content of that section is to be found in Matt. 24 and Mark 13.

2 Ezek. 9:3 (the same information in 10:4); 10:18–19; 11:22–23. The glory of God moves first from above the cherubim in the Holy of Holies to the threshold of the temple, then to the entrance of the east gate of the temple, and finally from there to 'the mountain that is on the east side of the city', which was later known as the Mount of Olives.

3 Matthew uses this word (*thlipsis* in Greek) three times in this chapter: here and in vv. 21 and 29. These last two are paralleled by Mark in Mark 13:19 and 24. The word occurs frequently in the New Testament to refer to the pain and suffering experienced as part of the normal Christian life—e.g. John 16:33; Rev. 1:9.

4 One fulfilment of this occurs in Acts 24–26, when Paul gives his testimony before two governors (Felix and Festus) and a king (Agrippa). Acts 25:10–12 points to the probability that Paul would appear before the Emperor Nero beyond the end of Acts.

5 Dan. 8:13; 9:27; 11:31; 12:11. While the first and third of these verses relate solely to Antiochus IV Epiphanes, the other two possibly refer to a figure in the much more distant future—the Antichrist, also to be identified as Paul's 'man of lawlessness' in 2 Thes. 2:3ff.—who will be in the mould of Antiochus IV Epiphanes but to a far more terrible degree.

6 Strictly speaking, Matt. 25:31–46 (the last part of this sequence of five episodes) is *not* a parable, unlike the first four. This will be explained in due course.

7 E.g. this has already been hinted at in Matt. 24:14 (Mark 13:10). See also Matt. 5:12; 28:19; Acts 1:8; Col. 4:5–6; 1 Peter 3:15.

The coming kingdom

(MATTHEW 25:1–46)

Introduction

Only Matthew includes the three well-known sections of this chapter. As was pointed out a little earlier, it might be better to regard them as a continuation of a series of *five* passages, beginning with the two in Matthew 24:43–44 and 45–51, on the subject of being prepared for Christ's Second Coming. There is no indication of any divide between Matthew chapters 24 and 25.

The Parable of the Ten Virgins (Matt. 25:1–13)

As in the earlier parable of the wedding feast in Matthew's Gospel, Jesus speaks of his relationship with his people as that of a bridegroom, and it was noted then that this image is drawn from Old Testament teaching about the relationship of God to his people and that the New Testament makes full use of this picture to describe Christ and his church.[1] When Jesus returns, he will take his followers to a celebration. This is by no means the normal way people by and large think of heaven, if they think of it at all.

In this parable we do not meet the bride. Instead, a group of five wise bridesmaids, who were prepared for the bridegroom's coming, are those who represent faithful Christians, ready for Christ's return. While the ten bridesmaids looked equally qualified for their duty, there was in fact as sharp a division between them as that between the two men in the field and the two women grinding at the mill in Jesus' earlier teaching (Matt. 24:40–41).

In approaching this parable, it is helpful to be aware that weddings in Jewish society of that time were conducted rather differently from those in our culture. First, there was the engagement—and later on the betrothal, which was regarded as binding. The betrothal period lasted for about a year, and at that point the bridegroom went to fetch his bride from her father's house and brought her back in procession to his own home, where the marriage feast was held.

The ten girls in Jesus' story were going to meet this procession. They did not know the exact time of the bridegroom's arrival, and he was delayed in his journey, with the result that they all fell asleep in the process of waiting. Some commentators suggest that the bridesmaids were at fault in falling asleep, and the command to 'stay awake' towards the end of the previous chapter of Matthew might seem to give weight to this comment. But in the context of this story, the difference between the two groups of bridesmaids becomes apparent in a different way. We should have some sympathy with the bridesmaids in their prolonged wait, and we should be honest enough to know that there are times when we are not as fired up and ready as we would like to be in our better moments.

The key point is that when the cry went up at midnight that the bridegroom was about to arrive, the truth was revealed concerning the ten bridesmaids. Five of them were ready, and five were woefully ill-prepared. Five of them had oil for their lamps, while the other five had none. It was useless for the foolish five to request oil for their lamps from their wise companions—there was none to spare. It was equally useless for them to go out in the middle of the night to try to purchase oil—while they were on their way, the bridegroom arrived. The one group of five bridesmaids joined the procession and went to the marriage feast, but the other group missed out. There is a chilling note in the story as this second group reached the house where the feast was taking place. The door was shut. In words which echo part of the conclusion to Jesus' Sermon on the Mount (Matt. 7:21–23), they cried out, 'Lord, lord, open to us.' The bridegroom, however, replied, 'Truly, I say to you, I do not know you.'

In fact, the application of this parable is not altogether different from the point that Jesus was making when he delivered his Sermon on that earlier occasion. What will count on that final day, when he comes again, is not our profession of orthodox beliefs (such as calling Jesus 'Lord'); nor is it our enthusiasm (not just calling him 'Lord', but saying, 'Lord, Lord!'); nor is it our claim to have an impressive track record in our Christian lives (even being able to claim that we have done impressive deeds in his name). Rather, what will count will be our obedience. He says, 'Not everyone who says to me, "Lord, Lord", will enter the kingdom of heaven, but the one who does the will of my Father who is in heaven' (Matt. 7:21). It is one thing to say that we believe in Jesus' Second Coming, as we may do regularly whenever we say the words of the Apostles' Creed or the Nicene Creed—but whether our lives are lived in active obedience to the Father's will made known to us in the plain teaching of the Bible is another matter. We show we are ready for the Lord's return by maintaining a close walk with him on a daily basis and seeking by his Spirit to please him in all we do.

The above paragraph represents the way we should apply the specific command of Jesus at the end of this parable: 'Watch therefore, for you know neither the day nor the hour.'

The Parable of the Talents (Matt. 25:14–30)

The Parable of the Talents is similar to a parable recorded by Luke which is normally known as the Parable of the Ten Minas. But there are certain differences between the two, and the one recorded by Luke is specifically set in the context of Jesus' journey towards Jerusalem, shortly before the Triumphal Entry (Luke 19:11–27).

The Parable of the Talents divides into three parts.

First, there is *the entrusting of the talents* to his servants by the master of a household before he went away on a journey. A talent, as explained in a footnote in many Bibles, was a unit of monetary reckoning (but not an actual coin) worth about twenty years' wages for a labourer. The sums of money in this story, therefore, were quite considerable. We are told about three of the servants, who received respectively five talents, two talents and one talent. The amounts, we are told, were reckoned to each servant 'according to his ability'. It would be tempting to interpret the talents in the parable as being what we today describe as 'talents'—in other words, our natural gifts and aptitudes. It would be better, however, to understand them to represent *everything* that the Lord entrusts to us. While this will include our talents (in our modern sense), it includes also our money, our time, our opportunities for Christian service—our whole lives. All these things belong to God, and not to us. We are stewards, of whom an account will one day—when Christ, our Master, returns—be required.

Second, there is *the reward of the faithful*. On his return, the master settled accounts with his servants. Both the servant entrusted with five talents and the servant entrusted with two talents had carried out their tasks faithfully. They had been fruitful in their master's service. As a result, they were rewarded by being given further and greater responsibilities and by being welcomed into their master's 'joy'. In terms of the application of this part of the parable, we can be sure that it is the Lord's evaluation, and not ours, that matters when the final accounts are settled. He sees fruit which no one else notices, and he recognizes some so-called fruit as worthless and sham. The key quality that is commended in Jesus' parable is faithfulness, which will be rewarded at his return.

Third, there is *the judgment of the sluggard*. The third servant did nothing but hide his talent in the ground. His excuse revealed more about him than he might have expected. It revealed that he had no understanding of, and no love for, his master. He totally misrepresented his master's character. His answer also revealed his laziness. 'Slothful' is the word the master used. Even if his assessment of his master had been correct, the least he could have done would have been to invest the money entrusted to him on his master's behalf, but he had failed even to do that. As a result, the lazy servant's talent was given to the first servant in the story. This third servant does not represent a true believer but someone whose Christianity is mere pretence. He was thrown out, and the description of his punishment is the one that we have already seen Jesus using regularly in connection with hell.[2]

The recurring theme throughout Jesus' teaching on his Second Coming is the need to take steps *now*, so as to be prepared *then*. When he comes again, the truth will be revealed. Nothing will be hidden. And it will not be possible on that final day to put the clock back. Time will have been overtaken by eternity.

The Final Judgment (Matt. 25:31–46)

This section is sometimes described as 'The Parable of the Sheep and the Goats'. It was mentioned earlier that this final part of a sequence of five episodes which illustrate what it means to be prepared for Christ's Second Coming is *not* a parable. Parables often invite us to compare two things. The Parable of the Ten Virgins begins 'Then the kingdom of heaven will be *like* ten virgins', and the Parable of the Talents begins 'For it will be *like* a man going on a journey'. Some parables simply paint a word picture, as with the two short parables at the end of Matthew 24, and the invitation to make a comparison between two things is only implicit. By contrast, this concluding part of Matthew 25 is straightforward teaching about the coming of the Son of Man.

From start to finish, the focus is on the Son of Man, coming in his glory and sitting on his glorious throne. He will separate the people of the world into two groups, just as a shepherd separates sheep from goats. This is the one simile used in this passage, but that does not turn the passage into a parable. The reason for this description of people as 'sheep' or 'goats' is that Palestinian sheep and goats looked remarkably similar, at least superficially. When they needed to be separated, it was not an easy task. But when the Son of Man separates people into two groups on that final day, he will make no mistakes—he will not be deceived by superficial appearances.

What we have in these verses is a judgment scene before the throne of Christ the King. This is the end of the world: the Last Judgment. This is the description, in concrete terms, of a truly awesome event: the very last event in the history of the world. And it is not sheep and goats who are being judged, but people. The people are 'all the nations'. They are everybody who has ever lived (or will have ever lived) on earth. No one will be missing. In this passage we read the description of a credible—but awesome—event.

Again and again, Jesus has been spelling out the stark reality that there are two ways to live—and *only* two ways to live. There are the wise bridesmaids and there are the foolish bridesmaids; there are good and faithful servants, and there are wicked and slothful servants.[3] In this passage in Matthew 25, the one group of people (the 'blessed') are assured that they are inheritors of the kingdom prepared for them from the foundation of the world, while the other group (the 'cursed') are sent away into the eternal fire prepared for the devil and his angels.

These closing verses of Matthew 25 are often misunderstood. Some claim that they teach that those who serve the poor are thereby serving Christ in them or that social action is to be the main priority of the church. Any such understanding is immediately challenged by the surprise that the 'righteous' register on hearing the reason the King gives for them being called to enter into their inheritance. There was no thought on their part that, by carrying out these deeds of compassion and mercy, they were in any way earning their salvation. Such a thought did not enter into their reckoning at all. Anyway, the Bible nowhere teaches that anyone can be saved on that basis. Salvation can only ever be on the basis of God's grace to those who trust in Jesus dying in their place as Saviour (Eph. 2:8–9; 1 Peter 3:18).

There is, of course, a link between faith and works—which is that we are saved not *by* good works but *for* good works (Eph. 2:10, which, it should be noted, follows on immediately from the two verses noted above). This is, in fact, the same point that arises out of the earlier incident concerning Jesus' cleansing of the temple and the cursing of the fig tree. Jesus had looked in vain for 'fruit' in relation to the spiritual life of the heart of Israel, just as he had found no fruit on the fig tree which promised so much. John the Baptist had challenged the Pharisees and Sadducees to 'bear fruit in keeping with repentance' (Matt. 3:8). The temple was condemned, along with those associated with it, because its impressive spiritual activity was the equivalent of 'leaves' and not 'fruit'. In terms of the 'sheep' and the 'goats' of Matthew 25:32, the religious leaders may have looked like sheep, but in the separating process carried out by the Shepherd-King they would have found themselves among the goats.

The 'righteous' are those who have shown their love and allegiance to their King by their actions towards the King's subjects. In this passage Jesus describes the actions of the righteous in this way: 'Truly, I say to you, as you did it to one of the least of these my brothers, you did it to me.' We have to ask ourselves who the least of these brothers of the King are. Two earlier sayings of Jesus in Matthew's Gospel help us here. There is a reference in Matthew chapter 12 to Jesus' 'brothers': 'whoever does the will of my Father in heaven is my brother and sister and mother' (Matt. 12:50). And there is a reference to people described in terms approximating to 'the least of these' in Matthew chapter 10: 'And whoever gives one of these little ones even a cup of cold water because he is a disciple, truly, I say to you, he will by no means lose his reward' (Matt. 10:42).

We can put all this together by saying that the criterion that King Jesus will use as a basis for judgment is whether we accept and love him. This is the 'fruit' which the Lord looks for and which is revealed in the lives of those whose hearts have been changed. Whether we accept him and love him is revealed not so much by what we say or profess, but by how much we love and care for fellow believers, especially those in need. Fellow believers in need will include those who bring the gospel message to us, because in many cultures they are the ones who are thrown into prison or are struggling in poverty. Jesus says elsewhere: 'Truly, truly, I say to you, whoever receives the one I send receives me, and whoever receives me receives the one who sent me' (John 13:20).

Prayer

Lord Jesus Christ,

You are THE KING, *who will sit on your glorious throne when you come in your glory.*

We thank you that you will take your people to join in the marriage feast of heaven, to enter into your joy and to inherit the kingdom prepared for them from the foundation of the world.

We ask you to keep us walking with you day by day, serving you faithfully and showing practical loving care to fellow believers. Amen.

NOTES

1 Matt. 22:1–14, discussed in Chapter 3 of this study. For examples of Old Testament references to God as the husband of his people, see Isa. 62:4–5; Hosea 2:16–20. For Jesus as the bridegroom of his people, see Matt. 9:15; John 3:29; Eph. 5.25–32; Rev. 21:2, 9.

2 Matt. 8:12; 13:42, 50; 22:13; 24:51; 25:30 (here).

3 See Matt. 7:13–14: there are two groups of people (the few and the many), two gates (the narrow and the wide), two roads (the hard and the easy) and two destinations (destruction and life).

The Saviour of the world

(JOHN 12:20–50)

Setting the scene

J ohn's Gospel has not been visited since the first chapter of this study. John does not include any of the action and speech recorded by the three Synoptic Gospel writers which took place following Jesus' Triumphal Entry into Jerusalem. But in the rest of chapter 12 of his Gospel, John does incorporate an account of some of Jesus' ministry, not to be found in the other three Gospels, that took place during the period of time between the Triumphal Entry and the evening of Maundy Thursday. The difficulty in pinpointing exactly when the activity of the rest of this chapter of John took place was discussed in the Introduction. There are three possibilities:

- It could be that everything in these verses took place immediately after Jesus' arrival in the capital on the Sunday.
- A second possibility is that these verses record what happened a few days later that week, following the events reported by the three Synoptic Gospel writers. The possibility that it could have been the Wednesday was tentatively suggested in the Introduction. The desire by some Greeks to meet Jesus, which in John chapter 12 is recorded just after the account of the Triumphal Entry, could possibly have been fuelled by their seeing and hearing Jesus in action in Jerusalem as recorded by the Synoptic Gospel writers. If that is correct, this would count as an argument for reckoning on there being a gap of time, even a few days, between verse 19 and verse 20 of John chapter 12.
- A third alternative is that John is recording events that took place on different days within that period of time.

We simply do not know, and it really does not matter at all that we cannot say for certain how the content of John 12:20–50 relates to the events of these few days recorded in the other three Gospels.

The Saviour of the world

The title of the current chapter of this study, 'The Saviour of the world', is drawn from an earlier incident in John's Gospel, when people from a town in Samaria, whom the Jews would have regarded as foreigners, came to faith in Jesus and acknowledged him as 'the Saviour of the world' (John 4:42). 'The world' is an important theme throughout John's Gospel.[1] For example, John spells out that the world was made through Jesus, the eternal Word, and yet 'the world did not know him', in the sense that mankind wilfully turned its back on its Creator (John 1:10). Nevertheless, in the words of perhaps the best-known verse in the Bible, 'God so loved the world, that he gave his only Son'—giving him to be 'the Lamb of God, who takes away the sin of the world' (John 3:16; 1:29).

This theme of Jesus as the Saviour of the world is particularly prominent in John chapter 12. In Chapter 1 of this study, we noticed—at the end of the section on John chapter 12 concerning the Triumphal Entry—the Pharisees' comment about 'the world' having gone after Jesus (John 12:19). As indicated in that earlier part of the study, John intends us, his readers, to understand that Jesus' enemies spoke more truly than they realized. What they meant as a negative assessment of Jesus' popular appeal was in fact an accurate statement about God's purpose that many from 'the world' should believe in Jesus and follow him.

In the course of the remainder of John chapter 12 we shall see:

- some Greeks, as representatives of the wider 'world', seeking Jesus (John 12:20ff.);
- the alternatives of loving life in 'this world' (which results in losing it) or hating it (which is the way to keep it for eternal life) (John 12:25);

- an announcement of judgment on the 'world' and the overthrow of its ruler, who is Satan—this will coincide with Jesus drawing people of all nations to himself through his crucifixion, which is at the same time his enthronement (John 12:31–32);
- a statement of Jesus' coming into the world as light and as Saviour (John 12:46–47).

Some Greeks seek Jesus (John 12:20–26)

The Greeks who wanted to see Jesus were probably converts to Judaism, or, to use the technical expression, they were Jewish proselytes. Like large numbers of Jewish believers from many parts of the Mediterranean world, they had come to Jerusalem for the Passover. Gentiles who became Jewish proselytes did so because they found the revealed religion of Judaism more satisfying than pagan superstitions. But these particular Greeks evidently found the appeal of Jesus even more satisfying.

One of the disciples, Philip, had a Greek name, which suggests that he might have been born in a Greek-speaking community.[2] Perhaps it was for this reason that the Greeks first approached Philip, who then cautiously asked for Andrew's advice. Together, they went to Jesus, and we assume that they introduced the enquiring Greeks to him.

The arrival of these Greeks—a small sample of 'the world' which had 'gone after' Jesus, in the words of the Pharisees—triggered a significant moment in Jesus' ministry, as he announced, 'The hour has come for the Son of Man to be glorified.' John has recorded Jesus using the term 'the hour' a number of times to refer to his forthcoming death on the cross (John 2:4; 4:21, 23; 7:30; 8:20). Each time until this point Jesus had been saying that 'the hour' had not yet arrived. Now, however, the event for which Jesus had come to earth was on the immediate horizon: 'the hour *has* come'. From the human perspective, crucifixion would look like ignominy and disgrace, but the true understanding of the cross is that it would mean his glorification.

Jesus went on to explain the significance of his death. It was the way to life—for himself and for those who trust in him—just as a grain of wheat seemingly has to die, when it is buried in the ground, before it produces a harvest (or 'bears much fruit'). Paul was to develop this picture later on, when he described Christ's resurrection from the dead as 'the firstfruits of those who have fallen asleep' (1 Cor. 15:20). The resurrection of Christian believers to eternal life will be the full harvest which Jesus' own death and his resurrection will produce. The implication of Greeks seeking Jesus is that this harvest will include Gentiles. And that implication will be made more explicit in a few verses' time (John 12:32). We have already seen indications in Jesus' teaching that membership of the kingdom would be extended to Gentiles.[3]

Jesus also explained how his disciples need to grasp this life-through-death principle. They are called to die to self and to live for Christ. If their love for Christ is such that, in comparison, their love for themselves in this world is like hatred, they can be assured that they will enjoy God's gift of eternal life.

The Son of Man must be lifted up (John 12:27–36a)

Jesus went on to speak more about his forthcoming death, and he did so in a very striking way: 'Now is my soul troubled.' 'Troubled' conveys shock and revulsion. It is an amazing glimpse of Jesus' real humanity alongside his divinity. Matthew, Mark and Luke show us exactly the same truth in their description of Jesus' agony in the Garden of Gethsemane, when his soul was 'very sorrowful, even to death', and he prayed earnestly that the cup of God's wrath, which he was to drink to the full on the cross, might pass from him (Matt. 26:38–39; Mark 14:34–35; Luke 22:42, 44).

In most Bible versions the next words of Jesus in John's account are in the form of two questions: 'And what shall I say? "Father, save me from this hour"?' However, punctuation marks are not part of the original text. It is possible, therefore, that the last part of the above Bible quotation should be in the form of a petition, not a question: 'Father, save me from this hour!' If that is the correct reading, this would make it a direct parallel of what the other Gospel writers record Jesus praying in the Garden. It was not the fear of *physical* death that Jesus was expressing in asking to be spared 'the hour' of the cross (or the cup of God's wrath). Rather, it was the horror and revulsion that the sinless Son of God experienced when he stared at the *spiritual* death involved in bearing the full measure of the Father's judgment on the accumulated mass of the sins of the whole world (and from all centuries, both BC and AD) that would be laid on his shoulders—the experience of being separated from his Father, with whom he had enjoyed unbroken fellowship from eternity.

Here in John chapter 12, as in the Synoptic Gospel writers' accounts of Jesus in the Garden, Jesus—amazingly—cancelled his own request. On the Thursday evening Jesus would pray: 'Yet not what I will, but what you will' (Matt. 26:39; Mark 14:36; Luke 22:42). Jesus' words in John chapter 12 were 'But for this purpose I have come to this hour. Father, glorify your name.' It was only the cross of Calvary that would declare the glory of God. It is not surprising that such a prayer, expressing the full obedience of the Son to the Father, was immediately answered from heaven: 'Then a voice came from heaven: "I have glorified it, and I will glorify it again."' According to Jesus, the Father's response was an audible witness for the benefit of the crowd. But many did not understand it, presumably because their hearts were not tuned in to understand the Father.

The world views the cross as a display of weakness and defeat. But Jesus taught here that the cross was a demonstration of power and victory. In the following verses, he said that the cross would achieve four things:

First, *the cross would pass judgment on the world*. Here is another instance of the recurring theme of 'the world'—and so often this word in

John's Gospel carries the nuance of mankind in rebellion against God. It is true that, when Jesus hung on the cross, the judgment of God on sin fell on him. But the cross exposed the sin of the human race in their rejection of their Creator and Lord in a way that declared them to be guilty and without excuse. Those who do not look to Jesus as the one who took the place of the guilty as their substitute must bear that judgment themselves.

Second, *the cross would pass judgment on Satan*. He is 'the ruler of this world' who would be cast out. Satan is not the ruler of this world by right: he is a usurper. The message of the cross seemed to be 'Jesus defeated'. But the real message of the cross is 'Jesus defeated Satan.' Satan's power still appears to be very evident in the world today, but his rule is at an end—his days are numbered; and one day, at Christ's return, he will be finally destroyed.

Third, *the cross would exalt Jesus*. Jesus referred to himself being 'lifted up'. This points to his being lifted up on the cross, as John explains: 'He said this to show by what kind of death he was going to die.' But the word used also points to Jesus being 'lifted up' in exaltation.[4] It is deliberately ambiguous. The cross would be Jesus' throne, and the crucifixion his coronation. Jesus reigns from the tree.

Fourth, *the cross is the means by which Jesus would draw all people to himself*. 'All people' is not meant in a universalistic sense, as if all will be saved. Rather, the meaning is 'all kinds of people', not just Jews but people from the wider world. At the start of this chapter we saw that John chapter 4, with its account of Jesus' ministry in Samaria, pointed to a worldwide harvest, as Samaritans believed in Jesus and hailed him as 'Saviour of the world'.[5] In the previous section of John chapter 12, we saw Greeks seeking Jesus: the firstfruits of the world who would go after him.

In this short section of John's Gospel Jesus made some amazing claims which challenged his hearers to a response. The surprise is that the response was very low-key. All that happened was that the crowd asked a further question, albeit a profound one: 'We have heard from the Law that the Christ remains for ever. How can you say that the Son of Man must be lifted up? Who is this Son of Man?' The difficulty being expressed seems to have to do with believing in a crucified Messiah. They understood that the title that Jesus used, 'the Son of Man', referred to the Messiah. Also, they understood that 'lifted up' referred to dying. But they could not grasp that the Messiah could possibly die, which is why they affirmed the Old Testament's teaching that 'the Christ remains for ever'.[6] Nor could they accept that Jesus could really be talking about himself—hence their question about the identity of the Son of Man. Jesus gave a gracious reply to the crowd. His answer was in effect that, if only people were willing to learn from him in the short time while he was still with them, he would give them the light of understanding and take away the darkness of their ignorance. It is only as anyone looks to Christ and listens to him that they can understand the significance of the cross and can find sufficient light to walk in his way.

The unbelief of the people (John 12:36b–43)

This section of John chapter 12 consists of comments by the Apostle John, incorporating two significant quotations from Isaiah. Jesus had withdrawn from the crowds for a while and would make one further speech in the final part of the chapter.

The issue that John focuses on is the unbelief of the people.

It would appear that Jesus' own assessment of the crowd's response to what he had been saying in the preceding section was far from positive. The low-key nature of the crowd's response to Jesus' claims about himself has already been commented on, and it seems that Jesus' reply to the crowd's question had not led to people wanting to follow him. This is in marked contrast to popular acclaim earlier in John chapter 12 (following the Triumphal Entry) and the response of faith, as it would appear to have been, on the part of the Greeks who wished to see Jesus.

There is no disguising John's surprise here that, despite hearing Jesus' teaching and seeing his miracles (described here, as elsewhere in John, as 'signs'), people persisted in unbelief. John's conclusion is that there were two reasons for this, namely God's sovereignty and human responsibility. We always find it difficult to hold on to both of these truths at the same time, because they seem to be mutually irreconcilable. But the Bible consistently affirms both. While God is sovereign and therefore fully and absolutely in control, men and women are accountable to God and fully responsible for their deeds.

First, *God's sovereignty*. John quotes two short passages from Isaiah, one from chapter 53 (53:1), the other from chapter 6 (6:10), both of which support the case that God wills the rejection of the truth by many. The first quotation comes from the passage about the Suffering Servant, and John introduces the quotation by saying that the people's unbelief took place in order to fulfil Isaiah's prophecy. This Old Testament verse tells us that people are not going to believe what they have heard from God's messenger (which, in the context of John chapter 12, points to the teaching of Jesus); nor are they going to believe that 'the arm of the Lord' is at work (in this context, pointing to the miraculous signs of Jesus). The second quotation comes from the passage about God's commission to the prophet to speak God's message and to do so in the full knowledge that people will not respond, because God himself will have blinded their eyes and hardened their hearts so that they will not believe. Isaiah's ministry would appear to be fruitless, confirming the people in their steady course towards judgment.[7] This is not arbitrary action on the part of God; it is an act of judgment on those who are determined to resist him. Of course, God acts in grace to enable and build up the faith of those who do believe, but he also acts to confirm the rejection of those who choose the path of unbelief. This is what was happening with those who heard Jesus' words that day in Jerusalem and failed to believe in him.

John adds the comment that 'Isaiah said these things because he saw his glory and spoke of him.' This is an amazing statement. John is telling us that when Isaiah, in his famous vision of Isaiah chapter 6, 'saw the Lord sitting upon a throne, high and lifted up', it was Jesus in his pre-incarnate glory whom he saw. This means also that it was Jesus who spoke those words to Isaiah about the effects of his words on his hearers, confirming them in the hardness of their hearts. But Isaiah also saw Jesus' glory in the Suffering Servant of chapter 53 of his book. As has already been noted, John's Gospel teaches that 'glory' and 'the cross' are virtually synonymous, because the glory of Jesus is to be seen in his saving death just as much as when he sits on his throne. Even on the cross, Jesus reigns as King.

Second, *human responsibility*. The final section of John chapter 12, to which we come shortly, will show us Jesus challenging people to put their faith in him, which would not make sense if there were no such thing as human responsibility. The last two verses of this present section of the chapter also spell this out. There were those who did believe, even among the authorities, and the implication is that more of the ordinary people believed than their leaders. However, the faith of these members of the hierarchy is somewhat questionable: it was secret discipleship, because they felt that the price to be paid for open allegiance to Jesus was too high. John makes a negative comment about these people: 'they loved the glory that comes from man more than the glory that comes from God'. They alone would have to bear the responsibility for their decision. The blame for the compromised nature of their discipleship could not be laid at God's door—it was fully theirs.

Jesus came to save the world (John 12:44–50)

In the closing verses of this chapter, John records one further brief address that Jesus delivered to the crowds. If the latter part of John chapter 12 does deal with what happened after the events of these few days in Jerusalem recorded by the Synoptic Gospel writers, these words of Jesus were his final public statement. As such, they carry an added significance and they form a fitting conclusion to the ministry of Jesus that has been examined in this study.

Jesus 'cried out' these words, John tells us. Presumably, his intention was that as many people as possible should hear what he had to say. Such was the importance of his words on this occasion. Of course, what Jesus spoke here was intended not only for those present in Jerusalem on that particular day, but for all succeeding generations—including ours today.

In these verses Jesus does four things:

He issues an appeal. The appeal to all who will listen is to believe in him and to look to him—and in so doing to discover that they are believing in, and looking to, the Father who has sent him. 'Believes' and 'sees' (or 'looks at' in the NIV) are used as parallel terms here. This second term is reminiscent of the incident of the bronze serpent in the wilderness, when those who wished to be cured of their snakebites needed to look at a bronze serpent, lifted up on a pole, in order to live.[8] Jesus is urging people to look trustingly to him, the one who—as he has explained earlier in this chapter—would himself be 'lifted up' on the cross as their substitute and sin-bearer.

He explains his mission. Jesus intends there to be no doubt about his true identity or his role on earth. He is no ordinary man. His origin is heaven: he has come from the Father, who sent him. He has come into 'the world'—another instance of that recurring theme in John chapter 12. 'The world', as has been noted earlier, is by definition hostile to God: the very opposite of heaven. But he has come in order 'to save the world'.

He presents a choice. A series of alternatives is laid out for us. The world is a place of 'darkness' but Jesus has come as 'light', so that people may pass from the former to the latter.[9] There are two alternatives—and only two alternatives—facing every human being: either to 'reject' Jesus or to 'receive' his words.[10] While Jesus has come to 'save' the world, those who ignore him will find that his words (i.e. the whole message of Jesus) 'judge' them on the Last Day when he comes again. Jesus spells out the truth of human responsibility, which was discussed in the previous section. Each of us will have to face up to the consequences of the fundamental choice we have made in this life.

He underlines the urgency. Judgment and salvation, or death and life, are eternal issues. The stakes could not be higher. Jesus closes his comments with what should be understood as offering a great encouragement to people to believe. He says, 'And I know that his commandment is eternal life.' The gospel message is a commandment. In its simplest form it is to 'repent' and 'believe' (Mark 1:15). But it is at the same time an invitation to receive 'eternal life', which means to know God as Father and Jesus Christ as Lord and Saviour (John 17:3). That eternal life begins here and now and continues even more wonderfully in the hereafter. Jesus speaks on his own—and his Father's—authority. These words carry a high priority and demand urgent attention.

Prayer

Lord Jesus Christ,

You are THE SAVIOUR OF THE WORLD, *who by your cross draw people of all nations to yourself.*

We thank you that, for the joy that was set before you, you endured the cross, despising the shame, and are seated at the right hand of the throne of God.

We ask that we may learn to die to our selfish selves and so keep our life for eternal life.

We thank you that you came into the world as light.

We ask that we may truly believe in you and not remain in darkness.

Give us a growing assurance that the words you have spoken carry the authority of the Father. Amen.

NOTES

1   It can be a useful exercise to explore, with the help of a good concordance, the nearly seventy occurrences of the word 'world' in John's Gospel.

2   According to John 1:44, Philip was from Bethsaida, a town in Galilee. The whole region of Galilee had a multinational character. It is described as 'Galilee of the Gentiles' in Matt. 4:15, part of Matthew's quotation from Isa. 9:1–2.

3   See earlier comments on Matt. 21:43 [Mark 12:9; Luke 20:16]; Matt. 22:8–9; Luke 21:24.

4   See John 3:14, where Jesus made use of the same deliberate double meaning of the word, which is explained by the following verses. See also John 8:28.

5   In John 10:16, Jesus, having called himself 'the good shepherd', anticipated bringing 'other sheep' (namely Gentiles) into the fold of God's people.

6   Peter had the same difficulty earlier in Jesus' ministry, when he recognized Jesus as the Christ but could not accept Jesus' teaching that the Son of Man 'must' be killed: Matt. 16:21–22; Mark 8:31–32.

7   Isa. 6:9–10 is also quoted in the New Testament in Matt. 13:14–15; Mark 4:12; Luke 8:10; and Acts 28:26–27.

8   Num. 21:4–9. Jesus refers to this incident in John 3:14; see note 4 above.

9   See John 5:24, where the invitation is to pass from death to life.

10 See Chapter 11 note 3.

The texts of the four Gospels from Palm Sunday to just before Maundy Thursday evening

CHAPTER 1: THE COMING OF THE KING

MATTHEW
The Triumphal Entry

21 Now when they drew near to Jerusalem and came to Bethphage, to the Mount of Olives, then Jesus sent two disciples, 2 saying to them, "Go into the village in front of you, and immediately you will find a donkey tied, and a colt with her. Untie them and bring them to me. 3 If anyone says anything to you, you shall say, 'The Lord needs them,' and he will send them at once." 4 This took place to fulfill what was spoken by the prophet, saying,

5 "Say to the daughter of Zion,
'Behold, your king is coming to you,
humble, and mounted on a donkey,
on a colt, the foal of a beast of burden.'"

6 The disciples went and did as Jesus had directed them. 7 They brought the donkey and the colt and put on them their cloaks, and he sat on them. 8 Most of the crowd spread their cloaks on the road, and others cut branches from the trees and spread them on the road. 9 And the crowds that went before him and that followed him were shouting, "Hosanna to the Son of David! Blessed is he who comes in the name of the Lord! Hosanna in the highest!" 10 And when he entered Jerusalem, the whole city was stirred up, saying, "Who is this?" 11 And the crowds said, "This is the prophet Jesus, from Nazareth of Galilee."

MARK
The Triumphal Entry

11 Now when they drew near to Jerusalem, to Bethphage and Bethany, at the Mount of Olives, Jesus sent two of his disciples 2 and said to them, "Go into the village in front of you, and immediately as you enter it you will find a colt tied, on which no one has ever sat. Untie it and bring it. 3 If anyone says to you, 'Why are you doing this?' say, 'The Lord has need of it and will send it back here immediately.' " 4 And they went away and found a colt tied at a door outside in the street, and they untied it. 5 And some of those standing there said to them, "What are you doing, untying the colt?" 6 And they told them what Jesus had said, and they let them go. 7 And they brought the colt to Jesus and threw their cloaks on it, and he sat on it. 8 And many spread their cloaks on the road, and others spread leafy branches that they had cut from the fields. 9 And those who went before and those who followed were shouting, "Hosanna! Blessed is he who comes in the name of the Lord! 10 Blessed is the coming kingdom of our father David! Hosanna in the highest!"

11 And he entered Jerusalem and went into the temple. And when he had looked around at everything, as it was already late, he went out to Bethany with the twelve.

LUKE
The Triumphal Entry

19:28 And when he had said these things, he went on ahead, going up to Jerusalem. **29** When he drew near to Bethphage and Bethany, at the mount that is called Olivet, he sent two of the disciples, **30** saying, "Go into the village in front of you, where on entering you will find a colt tied, on which no one has ever yet sat. Untie it and bring it here. **31** If anyone asks you, 'Why are you untying it?' you shall say this: 'The Lord has need of it.' " **32** So those who were sent went away and found it just as he had told them. **33** And as they were untying the colt, its owners said to them, "Why are you untying the colt?" **34** And they said, "The Lord has need of it." **35** And they brought it to Jesus, and throwing their cloaks on the colt, they set Jesus on it. **36** And as he rode along, they spread their cloaks on the road. **37** As he was drawing near—already on the way down the Mount of Olives—the whole multitude of his disciples began to rejoice and praise God with a loud voice for all the mighty works that they had seen, **38** saying, "Blessed is the King who comes in the name of the Lord! Peace in heaven and glory in the highest!" **39** And some of the Pharisees in the crowd said to him, "Teacher, rebuke your disciples." **40** He answered, "I tell you, if these were silent, the very stones would cry out."

Jesus Weeps over Jerusalem

41 And when he drew near and saw the city, he wept over it, **42** saying, "Would that you, even you, had known on this day the things that make for peace! But now they are hidden from your eyes. **43** For the days will come upon you, when your enemies will set up a barricade around you and surround you and hem you in on every side **44** and tear you down to the ground, you and your children within you. And they will not leave one stone upon another in you, because you did not know the time of your visitation."

JOHN
The Triumphal Entry

12:12 The next day the large crowd that had come to the feast heard that Jesus was coming to Jerusalem. **13** So they took branches of palm trees and went out to meet him, crying out, "Hosanna! Blessed is he who comes in the name of the Lord, even the King of Israel!" **14** And Jesus found a young donkey and sat on it, just as it is written,

15 "Fear not, daughter of Zion;
behold, your king is coming,
sitting on a donkey's colt!"

16 His disciples did not understand these things at first, but when Jesus was glorified, then they remembered that these things had been written about him and had been done to him. **17** The crowd that had been with him when he called Lazarus out of the tomb and raised him from the dead continued to bear witness. **18** The reason why the crowd went to meet him was that they heard he had done this sign. **19** So the Pharisees said to one another, "You see that you are gaining nothing. Look, the world has gone after him."

CHAPTER 2: THE FIG TREE AND THE TEMPLE

MATTHEW
Jesus Cleanses the Temple

12 And Jesus entered the temple and drove out all who sold and bought in the temple, and he overturned the tables of the money-changers and the seats of those who sold pigeons. **13** He said to them, "It is written, 'My house shall be called a house of prayer,' but you make it a den of robbers."

14 And the blind and the lame came to him in the temple, and he healed them. **15** But when the chief priests and the scribes saw the wonderful things that he did, and the children crying out in the temple, "Hosanna to the Son of David!" they were indignant, **16** and they said to him, "Do you hear what these are saying?" And Jesus said to them, "Yes; have you never read,

"'Out of the mouth of infants and nursing babies you have prepared praise'?"

17 And leaving them, he went out of the city to Bethany and lodged there.

Jesus Curses the Fig Tree

18 In the morning, as he was returning to the city, he became hungry. **19** And seeing a fig tree by the wayside, he went to it and found nothing on it but only leaves. And he said to it, "May no fruit ever come from you again!" And the fig tree withered at once.

20 When the disciples saw it, they marveled, saying, "How did the fig tree wither at once?" **21** And Jesus answered them, "Truly, I say to you, if you have faith and do not doubt, you will not only do what has been done to the fig tree, but even if you say to this mountain, 'Be taken up and thrown into the sea,' it will happen. **22** And whatever you ask in prayer, you will receive, if you have faith."

MARK
Jesus Curses the Fig Tree and Cleanses the Temple [I]

12 On the following day, when they came from Bethany, he was hungry. **13** And seeing in the distance a fig tree in leaf, he went to see if he could find anything on it. When he came to it, he found nothing but leaves, for it was not the season for figs. **14** And he said to it, "May no one ever eat fruit from you again." And his disciples heard it.

15 And they came to Jerusalem. And he entered the temple and began to drive out those who sold and those who bought in the temple, and he overturned the tables of the money-changers and the seats of those who sold pigeons. **16** And he would not allow anyone to carry anything through the temple. **17** And he was teaching them and saying to them, "Is it not written, 'My house shall be called a house of prayer for all the nations'? But you have made it a den of robbers." **18** And the chief priests and the scribes heard it and were seeking a way to destroy him, for they feared him, because all the crowd was astonished at his teaching. **19** And when evening came they went out of the city.

20 As they passed by in the morning, they saw the fig tree withered away to its roots. **21** And Peter remembered and said to him, "Rabbi, look! The fig tree that you cursed has withered." **22** And Jesus answered them, "Have faith in God. **23** Truly, I say to you, whoever says to this mountain, 'Be taken up and thrown into the sea,' and does not doubt in his heart, but believes that what he says will come to pass, it will be done for him. **24** Therefore I tell you, whatever you ask in prayer, believe that you have received it, and it will be yours. **25** And whenever you stand praying, forgive, if you have anything against anyone, so that your Father also who is in heaven may forgive you your trespasses."

LUKE

Jesus Cleanses the Temple

45 And he entered the temple and began to drive out those who sold, **46** saying to them, "It is written, 'My house shall be a house of prayer,' but you have made it a den of robbers."

47 And he was teaching daily in the temple. The chief priests and the scribes and the principal men of the people were seeking to destroy him, **48** but they did not find anything they could do, for all the people were hanging on his words.

CHAPTER 3: CHALLENGE 1—A QUESTION OF AUTHORITY

MATTHEW
The Authority of Jesus Challenged

23 And when he entered the temple, the chief priests and the elders of the people came up to him as he was teaching, and said, "By what authority are you doing these things, and who gave you this authority?" 24 Jesus answered them, "I also will ask you one question, and if you tell me the answer, then I also will tell you by what authority I do these things. 25 The baptism of John, from where did it come? From heaven or from man?" And they discussed it among themselves, saying, "If we say, 'From heaven,' he will say to us, 'Why then did you not believe him?' 26 But if we say, 'From man,' we are afraid of the crowd, for they all hold that John was a prophet." 27 So they answered Jesus, "We do not know." And he said to them, "Neither will I tell you by what authority I do these things.

The Parable of the Two Sons

28 "What do you think? A man had two sons. And he went to the first and said, 'Son, go and work in the vineyard today.' 29 And he answered, 'I will not,' but afterward he changed his mind and went. 30 And he went to the other son and said the same. And he answered, 'I go, sir,' but did not go. 31 Which of the two did the will of his father?" They said, "The first." Jesus said to them, "Truly, I say to you, the tax collectors and the prostitutes go into the kingdom of God before you. 32 For John came to you in the way of righteousness, and you did not believe him, but the tax collectors and the prostitutes believed him. And even when you saw it, you did not afterward change your minds and believe him.

MARK
The Authority of Jesus Challenged

27 And they came again to Jerusalem. And as he was walking in the temple, the chief priests and the scribes and the elders came to him, 28 and they said to him, "By what authority are you doing these things, or who gave you this authority to do them?" 29 Jesus said to them, "I will ask you one question; answer me, and I will tell you by what authority I do these things. 30 Was the baptism of John from heaven or from man? Answer me." 31 And they discussed it with one another, saying, "If we say, 'From heaven,' he will say, 'Why then did you not believe him?' 32 But shall we say, 'From man'?"—they were afraid of the people, for they all held that John really was a prophet. 33 So they answered Jesus, "We do not know." And Jesus said to them, "Neither will I tell you by what authority I do these things."

LUKE
The Authority of Jesus Challenged

20 *One day, as Jesus was teaching the people in the temple and preaching the gospel, the chief priests and the scribes with the elders came up* **2** *and said to him, "Tell us by what authority you do these things, or who it is that gave you this authority."* **3** *He answered them, "I also will ask you a question. Now tell me,* **4** *was the baptism of John from heaven or from man?"* **5** *And they discussed it with one another, saying, "If we say, 'From heaven,' he will say, 'Why did you not believe him?'* **6** *But if we say, 'From man,' all the people will stone us to death, for they are convinced that John was a prophet."* **7** *So they answered that they did not know where it came from.* **8** *And Jesus said to them, "Neither will I tell you by what authority I do these things."*

MATTHEW
The Parable of the Tenants

33 "Hear another parable. There was a master of a house who planted a vineyard and put a fence around it and dug a winepress in it and built a tower and leased it to tenants, and went into another country. **34** When the season for fruit drew near, he sent his servants to the tenants to get his fruit. **35** And the tenants took his servants and beat one, killed another, and stoned another. **36** Again he sent other servants, more than the first. And they did the same to them. **37** Finally he sent his son to them, saying, 'They will respect my son.' **38** But when the tenants saw the son, they said to themselves, 'This is the heir. Come, let us kill him and have his inheritance.' **39** And they took him and threw him out of the vineyard and killed him. **40** When therefore the owner of the vineyard comes, what will he do to those tenants?" **41** They said to him, "He will put those wretches to a miserable death and let out the vineyard to other tenants who will give him the fruits in their seasons."

42 Jesus said to them, "Have you never read in the Scriptures:

"'The stone that the builders rejected
has become the cornerstone;
this was the Lord's doing,
and it is marvelous in our eyes'?

43 Therefore I tell you, the kingdom of God will be taken away from you and given to a people producing its fruits. **44** And the one who falls on this stone will be broken to pieces; and when it falls on anyone, it will crush him."

45 When the chief priests and the Pharisees heard his parables, they perceived that he was speaking about them. **46** And although they were seeking to arrest him, they feared the crowds, because they held him to be a prophet.

MARK
The Parable of the Tenants

12 And he began to speak to them in parables. "A man planted a vineyard and put a fence around it and dug a pit for the winepress and built a tower, and leased it to tenants and went into another country. **2** When the season came, he sent a servant to the tenants to get from them some of the fruit of the vineyard. **3** And they took him and beat him and sent him away empty-handed. **4** Again he sent to them another servant, and they struck him on the head and treated him shamefully. **5** And he sent another, and him they killed. And so with many others: some they beat, and some they killed. **6** He had still one other, a beloved son. Finally he sent him to them, saying, 'They will respect my son.' **7** But those tenants said to one another, 'This is the heir. Come, let us kill him, and the inheritance will be ours.' **8** And they took him and killed him and threw him out of the vineyard. **9** What will the owner of the vineyard do? He will come and destroy the tenants and give the vineyard to others. **10** Have you not read this Scripture:

"'The stone that the builders rejected
has become the cornerstone;
11 this was the Lord's doing,
and it is marvelous in our eyes'?"

12 And they were seeking to arrest him but feared the people, for they perceived that he had told the parable against them. So they left him and went away.

LUKE
The Parable of the Tenants[2]

9 And he began to tell the people this parable: "A man planted a vineyard and let it out to tenants and went into another country for a long while. **10** When the time came, he sent a servant to the tenants, so that they would give him some of the fruit of the vineyard. But the tenants beat him and sent him away empty-handed. **11** And he sent another servant. But they also beat and treated him shamefully, and sent him away empty-handed. **12** And he sent yet a third. This one also they wounded and cast out. **13** Then the owner of the vineyard said, 'What shall I do? I will send my beloved son; perhaps they will respect him.' **14** But when the tenants saw him, they said to themselves, 'This is the heir. Let us kill him, so that the inheritance may be ours.' **15** And they threw him out of the vineyard and killed him. What then will the owner of the vineyard do to them? **16** He will come and destroy those tenants and give the vineyard to others." When they heard this, they said, "Surely not!" **17** But he looked directly at them and said, "What then is this that is written:

"'The stone that the builders rejected
has become the cornerstone'?

18 Everyone who falls on that stone will be broken to pieces, and when it falls on anyone, it will crush him."

MATTHEW
The Parable of the Wedding Feast

22 And again Jesus spoke to them in parables, saying, **2** "The kingdom of heaven may be compared to a king who gave a wedding feast for his son, **3** and sent his servants to call those who were invited to the wedding feast, but they would not come. **4** Again he sent other servants, saying, 'Tell those who are invited, "See, I have prepared my dinner, my oxen and my fat calves have been slaughtered, and everything is ready. Come to the wedding feast." ' **5** But they paid no attention and went off, one to his farm, another to his business, **6** while the rest seized his servants, treated them shamefully, and killed them. **7** The king was angry, and he sent his troops and destroyed those murderers and burned their city. **8** Then he said to his servants, 'The wedding feast is ready, but those invited were not worthy. **9** Go therefore to the main roads and invite to the wedding feast as many as you find.' **10** And those servants went out into the roads and gathered all whom they found, both bad and good. So the wedding hall was filled with guests.

11 "But when the king came in to look at the guests, he saw there a man who had no wedding garment. **12** And he said to him, 'Friend, how did you get in here without a wedding garment?' And he was speechless. **13** Then the king said to the attendants, 'Bind him hand and foot and cast him into the outer darkness. In that place there will be weeping and gnashing of teeth.' **14** For many are called, but few are chosen."

CHAPTER 4: CHALLENGE 2—A QUESTION OF ALLEGIANCE

MATTHEW
Paying Taxes to Caesar

15 Then the Pharisees went and plotted how to entangle him in his words. **16** And they sent their disciples to him, along with the Herodians, saying, "Teacher, we know that you are true and teach the way of God truthfully, and you do not care about anyone's opinion, for you are not swayed by appearances. **17** Tell us, then, what you think. Is it lawful to pay taxes to Caesar, or not?" **18** But Jesus, aware of their malice, said, "Why put me to the test, you hypocrites? **19** Show me the coin for the tax." And they brought him a denarius. **20** And Jesus said to them, "Whose likeness and inscription is this?" **21** They said, "Caesar's." Then he said to them, "Therefore render to Caesar the things that are Caesar's, and to God the things that are God's." **22** When they heard it, they marveled. And they left him and went away.

MARK
Paying Taxes to Caesar

13 And they sent to him some of the Pharisees and some of the Herodians, to trap him in his talk. **14** And they came and said to him, "Teacher, we know that you are true and do not care about anyone's opinion. For you are not swayed by appearances, but truly teach the way of God. Is it lawful to pay taxes to Caesar, or not? Should we pay them, or should we not?" **15** But, knowing their hypocrisy, he said to them, "Why put me to the test? Bring me a denarius and let me look at it." **16** And they brought one. And he said to them, "Whose likeness and inscription is this?" They said to him, "Caesar's." **17** Jesus said to them, "Render to Caesar the things that are Caesar's, and to God the things that are God's." And they marveled at him.

LUKE
Paying Taxes to Caesar

19 *The scribes and the chief priests sought to lay hands on him at that very hour, for they perceived that he had told this parable against them, but they feared the people.* **20** *So they watched him and sent spies, who pretended to be sincere, that they might catch him in something he said, so as to deliver him up to the authority and jurisdiction of the governor.* **21** *So they asked him, "Teacher, we know that you speak and teach rightly, and show no partiality, but truly teach the way of God.* **22** *Is it lawful for us to give tribute to Caesar, or not?"* **23** *But he perceived their craftiness, and said to them,* **24** *"Show me a denarius. Whose likeness and inscription does it have?" They said, "Caesar's."* **25** *He said to them, "Then render to Caesar the things that are Caesar's, and to God the things that are God's."* **26** *And they were not able in the presence of the people to catch him in what he said, but marveling at his answer they became silent.*

CHAPTER 5: CHALLENGE 3—A QUESTION OF LIFE AND DEATH

MATTHEW
Sadducees Ask About the Resurrection

23 The same day Sadducees came to him, who say that there is no resurrection, and they asked him a question, **24** saying, "Teacher, Moses said, 'If a man dies having no children, his brother must marry the widow and raise up offspring for his brother.' **25** Now there were seven brothers among us. The first married and died, and having no offspring left his wife to his brother. **26** So too the second and third, down to the seventh. **27** After them all, the woman died. **28** In the resurrection, therefore, of the seven, whose wife will she be? For they all had her."

29 But Jesus answered them, "You are wrong, because you know neither the Scriptures nor the power of God. **30** For in the resurrection they neither marry nor are given in marriage, but are like angels in heaven. **31** And as for the resurrection of the dead, have you not read what was said to you by God: **32** 'I am the God of Abraham, and the God of Isaac, and the God of Jacob'? He is not God of the dead, but of the living." **33** And when the crowd heard it, they were astonished at his teaching.

MARK
Sadducees Ask About the Resurrection[3]

18 And Sadducees came to him, who say that there is no resurrection. And they asked him a question, saying, **19** "Teacher, Moses wrote for us that if a man's brother dies and leaves a wife, but leaves no child, the man must take the widow and raise up offspring for his brother. **20** There were seven brothers; the first took a wife, and when he died left no offspring. **21** And the second took her, and died, leaving no offspring. And the third likewise. **22** And the seven left no offspring. Last of all the woman also died. **23** In the resurrection, when they rise again, whose wife will she be? For the seven had her as wife."

24 Jesus said to them, "Is this not the reason you are wrong, because you know neither the Scriptures nor the power of God? **25** For when they rise from the dead, they neither marry nor are given in marriage, but are like angels in heaven. **26** And as for the dead being raised, have you not read in the book of Moses, in the passage about the bush, how God spoke to him, saying, 'I am the God of Abraham, and the God of Isaac, and the God of Jacob'? **27** He is not God of the dead, but of the living. You are quite wrong."

LUKE
Sadducees Ask About the Resurrection

27 There came to him some Sadducees, those who deny that there is a resurrection, **28** and they asked him a question, saying, "Teacher, Moses wrote for us that if a man's brother dies, having a wife but no children, the man must take the widow and raise up offspring for his brother. **29** Now there were seven brothers. The first took a wife, and died without children. **30** And the second **31** and the third took her, and likewise all seven left no children and died. **32** Afterward the woman also died. **33** In the resurrection, therefore, whose wife will the woman be? For the seven had her as wife."

34 And Jesus said to them, "The sons of this age marry and are given in marriage, **35** but those who are considered worthy to attain to that age and to the resurrection from the dead neither marry nor are given in marriage, **36** for they cannot die anymore, because they are equal to angels and are sons of God, being sons of the resurrection. **37** But that the dead are raised, even Moses showed, in the passage about the bush, where he calls the Lord the God of Abraham and the God of Isaac and the God of Jacob. **38** Now he is not God of the dead, but of the living, for all live to him." **39** Then some of the scribes answered, "Teacher, you have spoken well." **40** For they no longer dared to ask him any question.

CHAPTER 6: CHALLENGE 4—A QUESTION OF IMPORTANCE

MATTHEW
The Great Commandment

34 But when the Pharisees heard that he had silenced the Sadducees, they gathered together. **35** And one of them, a lawyer, asked him a question to test him. **36** "Teacher, which is the great commandment in the Law?" **37** And he said to him, "You shall love the Lord your God with all your heart and with all your soul and with all your mind. **38** This is the great and first commandment. **39** And a second is like it: You shall love your neighbor as yourself. **40** On these two commandments depend all the Law and the Prophets."

MARK
The Great Commandment

28 And one of the scribes came up and heard them disputing with one another, and seeing that he answered them well, asked him, "Which commandment is the most important of all?" **29** Jesus answered, "The most important is, 'Hear, O Israel: The Lord our God, the Lord is one. **30** And you shall love the Lord your God with all your heart and with all your soul and with all your mind and with all your strength.' **31** The second is this: 'You shall love your neighbor as yourself.' There is no other commandment greater than these." **32** And the scribe said to him, "You are right, Teacher. You have truly said that he is one, and there is no other besides him. **33** And to love him with all the heart and with all the understanding and with all the strength, and to love one's neighbor as oneself, is much more than all whole burnt offerings and sacrifices." **34** And when Jesus saw that he answered wisely, he said to him, "You are not far from the kingdom of God." And after that no one dared to ask him any more questions.

CHAPTER 7: CHALLENGE 5—JESUS ASKS A QUESTION

MATTHEW
Whose Son Is the Christ?

41 Now while the Pharisees were gathered together, Jesus asked them a question, **42** saying, "What do you think about the Christ? Whose son is he?" They said to him, "The son of David." **43** He said to them, "How is it then that David, in the Spirit, calls him Lord, saying,

44 "'The Lord said to my Lord,
"Sit at my right hand,
until I put your enemies under your feet"'?

45 If then David calls him Lord, how is he his son?" **46** And no one was able to answer him a word, nor from that day did anyone dare to ask him any more questions.

MARK
Whose Son Is the Christ?

35 And as Jesus taught in the temple, he said, "How can the scribes say that the Christ is the son of David? **36** David himself, in the Holy Spirit, declared,

"'The Lord said to my Lord,
"Sit at my right hand,
until I put your enemies under
your feet."'

37 David himself calls him Lord. So how is he his son?" And the great throng heard him gladly.

LUKE
Whose Son Is the Christ?

41 *But he said to them, "How can they say that the Christ is David's son? **42** For David himself says in the Book of Psalms,*

> *"'The Lord said to my Lord,*
> *"Sit at my right hand,*
43 *   until I make your enemies your footstool." '*
44 *David thus calls him Lord, so how is he his son?"*

CHAPTER 8: JUDGMENT ON HYPOCRITES

MATTHEW
Seven Woes to the Scribes and Pharisees

23 Then Jesus said to the crowds and to his disciples, **2** "The scribes and the Pharisees sit on Moses' seat, **3** so do and observe whatever they tell you, but not the works they do. For they preach, but do not practice. **4** They tie up heavy burdens, hard to bear, and lay them on people's shoulders, but they themselves are not willing to move them with their finger. **5** They do all their deeds to be seen by others. For they make their phylacteries broad and their fringes long, **6** and they love the place of honor at feasts and the best seats in the synagogues **7** and greetings in the marketplaces and being called rabbi by others. **8** But you are not to be called rabbi, for you have one teacher, and you are all brothers. **9** And call no man your father on earth, for you have one Father, who is in heaven. **10** Neither be called instructors, for you have one instructor, the Christ. **11** The greatest among you shall be your servant. **12** Whoever exalts himself will be humbled, and whoever humbles himself will be exalted.

13 "But woe to you, scribes and Pharisees, hypocrites! For you shut the kingdom of heaven in people's faces. For you neither enter yourselves nor allow those who would enter to go in. ^{4}

15 "Woe to you, scribes and Pharisees, hypocrites! For you travel across sea and land to make a single proselyte, and when he becomes a proselyte, you make him twice as much a child of hell as yourselves.

16 "Woe to you, blind guides, who say, 'If anyone swears by the temple, it is nothing, but if anyone swears by the gold of the temple, he is bound by his oath.' **17** You blind fools! For which is greater, the gold or the temple that has made the gold sacred? **18** And you say, 'If anyone swears by the altar, it is nothing, but if anyone swears by the gift that is on the altar, he is bound by his oath.' **19** You blind men! For which is greater, the gift or the altar that makes the gift sacred? **20** So whoever swears by the altar swears by it and by everything on it. **21** And whoever swears by the temple swears by it and by him who dwells in it. **22** And whoever swears by heaven swears by the throne of God and by him who sits upon it.

23 "Woe to you, scribes and Pharisees, hypocrites! For you tithe mint and dill and cumin, and have neglected the weightier matters of the law: justice and mercy and faithfulness. These you ought to have done, without neglecting the others. **24** You blind guides, straining out a gnat and swallowing a camel!

25 "Woe to you, scribes and Pharisees, hypocrites! For you clean the outside of the cup and the plate, but inside they are full of greed and self-indulgence. **26** You blind Pharisee! First clean the inside of the cup and the plate, that the outside also may be clean.

27 "Woe to you, scribes and Pharisees, hypocrites! For you are like whitewashed tombs, which outwardly appear beautiful, but within are full of dead people's bones and all uncleanness. **28** So you also outwardly appear righteous to others, but within you are full of hypocrisy and lawlessness.

29 "Woe to you, scribes and Pharisees, hypocrites! For you build the tombs of the prophets and decorate the monuments of the righteous, **30** saying, 'If we had lived in the days of our fathers, we would not have taken part with them in shedding the blood of the prophets.' **31** Thus you witness against yourselves that you are sons of those who murdered the prophets. **32** Fill up, then, the measure of your fathers. ⁵

33 "You serpents, you brood of vipers, how are you to escape being sentenced to hell? **34** Therefore I send you prophets and wise men and scribes, some of whom you will kill and crucify, and some you will flog in your synagogues and persecute from town to town, **35** so that on you may come all the righteous blood shed on earth, from the blood of righteous Abel to the blood of Zechariah the son of Barachiah, whom you murdered between the sanctuary and the altar. **36** Truly, I say to you, all these things will come upon this generation.

Lament over Jerusalem

37 "O Jerusalem, Jerusalem, the city that kills the prophets and stones those who are sent to it! How often would I have gathered your children together as a hen gathers her brood under her wings, and you were not willing! **38** See, your house is left to you desolate. **39** For I tell you, you will not see me again, until you say, 'Blessed is he who comes in the name of the Lord.' "

MARK
Beware of the Scribes

38 And in his teaching he said, "Beware of the scribes, who like to walk around in long robes and like greetings in the marketplaces **39** and have the best seats in the synagogues and the places of honour at feasts, **40** who devour widows' houses and for a pretense make long prayers. They will receive the greater condemnation."

LUKE
Beware of the Scribes

45 And in the hearing of all the people he said to his disciples, 46 "Beware of the scribes, who like to walk around in long robes, and love greetings in the marketplaces and the best seats in the synagogues and the places of honour at feasts, 47 who devour widows' houses and for a pretense make long prayers. They will receive the greater condemnation."

CHAPTER 9: AN EXAMPLE TO FOLLOW

MARK
The Widow's Offering
41 And he sat down opposite the treasury and watched the people putting money into the offering box. Many rich people put in large sums. 42 And a poor widow came and put in two small copper coins, which make a penny. 43 And he called his disciples to him and said to them, "Truly, I say to you, this poor widow has put in more than all those who are contributing to the offering box. 44 For they all contributed out of their abundance, but she out of her poverty has put in everything she had, all she had to live on."

LUKE
The Widow's Offering

21 Jesus looked up and saw the rich putting their gifts into the offering box, **2** and he saw a poor widow put in two small copper coins. **3** And he said, "Truly, I tell you, this poor widow has put in more than all of them. **4** For they all contributed out of their abundance, but she out of her poverty put in all she had to live on."

CHAPTER 10: BE PREPARED!

MATTHEW
Jesus' Foretelling of the Destruction of the Temple—and the Disciples' Questions[6]

24 Jesus left the temple and was going away, when his disciples came to point out to him the buildings of the temple. **2** But he answered them, "You see all these, do you not? Truly, I say to you, there will not be left here one stone upon another that will not be thrown down."

3 As he sat on the Mount of Olives, the disciples came to him privately, saying, "Tell us, when will these things be, and what will be the sign of your coming and of the end of the age?"

A Road-Map to the End (A)

4 And Jesus answered them, "See that no one leads you astray. **5** For many will come in my name, saying, 'I am the Christ,' and they will lead many astray. **6** And you will hear of wars and rumours of wars. See that you are not alarmed, for this must take place, but the end is not yet. **7** For nation will rise against nation, and kingdom against kingdom, and there will be famines and earthquakes in various places. **8** All these are but the beginning of the birth pains.

9 "Then they will deliver you up to tribulation and put you to death, and you will be hated by all nations for my name's sake. **10** And then many will fall away and betray one another and hate one another. **11** And many false prophets will arise and lead many astray. **12** And because lawlessness will be increased, the love of many will grow cold. **13** But the one who endures to the end will be saved. **14** And this gospel of the kingdom will be proclaimed throughout the whole world as a testimony to all nations, and then the end will come."

MARK
Jesus' Foretelling of the Destruction of the Temple—and the Disciples' Questions

13 And as he came out of the temple, one of his disciples said to him, "Look, Teacher, what wonderful stones and what wonderful buildings!" **2** And Jesus said to him, "Do you see these great buildings? There will not be left here one stone upon another that will not be thrown down."

3 And as he sat on the Mount of Olives opposite the temple, Peter and James and John and Andrew asked him privately, **4** "Tell us, when will these things be, and what will be the sign when all these things are about to be accomplished?"

A Road-Map to the End (A)

5 And Jesus began to say to them, "See that no one leads you astray. **6** Many will come in my name, saying, 'I am he!' and they will lead many astray. **7** And when you hear of wars and rumours of wars, do not be alarmed. This must take place, but the end is not yet. **8** For nation will rise against nation, and kingdom against kingdom. There will be earthquakes in various places; there will be famines. These are but the beginning of the birth pains.

9 "But be on your guard. For they will deliver you over to councils, and you will be beaten in synagogues, and you will stand before governors and kings for my sake, to bear witness before them. **10** And the gospel must first be proclaimed to all nations. **11** And when they bring you to trial and deliver you over, do not be anxious beforehand what you are to say, but say whatever is given you in that hour, for it is not you who speak, but the Holy Spirit. **12** And brother will deliver brother over to death, and the father his child, and children will rise against parents and have them put to death. **13** And you will be hated by all for my name's sake. But the one who endures to the end will be saved.

LUKE
Jesus' Foretelling of the Destruction of the Temple—and the Disciples' Questions

5 *And while some were speaking of the temple, how it was adorned with noble stones and offerings, he said,* **6** *"As for these things that you see, the days will come when there will not be left here one stone upon another that will not be thrown down."*

7 *And they asked him, "Teacher, when will these things be, and what will be the sign when these things are about to take place?"*

A Road-Map to the End

8 *And he said, "See that you are not led astray. For many will come in my name, saying, 'I am he!' and, 'The time is at hand!' Do not go after them.* **9** *And when you hear of wars and tumults, do not be terrified, for these things must first take place, but the end will not be at once."*

10 *Then he said to them, "Nation will rise against nation, and kingdom against kingdom.* **11** *There will be great earthquakes, and in various places famines and pestilences. And there will be terrors and great signs from heaven.* **12** *But before all this they will lay their hands on you and persecute you, delivering you up to the synagogues and prisons, and you will be brought before kings and governors for my name's sake.* **13** *This will be your opportunity to bear witness.* **14** *Settle it therefore in your minds not to meditate beforehand how to answer,* **15** *for I will give you a mouth and wisdom, which none of your adversaries will be able to withstand or contradict.* **16** *You will be delivered up even by parents and brothers and relatives and friends, and some of you they will put to death.* **17** *You will be hated by all for my name's sake.* **18** *But not a hair of your head will perish.* **19** *By your endurance you will gain your lives.*

MATTHEW
The Fall of Jerusalem[7]

15 "So when you see the abomination of desolation spoken of by the prophet Daniel, standing in the holy place (let the reader understand), **16** then let those who are in Judea flee to the mountains. **17** Let the one who is on the housetop not go down to take what is in his house, **18** and let the one who is in the field not turn back to take his cloak. **19** And alas for women who are pregnant and for those who are nursing infants in those days! **20** Pray that your flight may not be in winter or on a Sabbath. **21** For then there will be great tribulation, such as has not been from the beginning of the world until now, no, and never will be.

A Road-Map to the End (B)

22 "And if those days had not been cut short, no human being would be saved. But for the sake of the elect those days will be cut short. **23** Then if anyone says to you, 'Look, here is the Christ!' or 'There he is!' do not believe it. **24** For false christs and false prophets will arise and perform great signs and wonders, so as to lead astray, if possible, even the elect. **25** See, I have told you beforehand. **26** So, if they say to you, 'Look, he is in the wilderness,' do not go out. If they say, 'Look, he is in the inner rooms,' do not believe it. **27** For as the lightning comes from the east and shines as far as the west, so will be the coming of the Son of Man. **28** Wherever the corpse is, there the vultures will gather.

MARK
The Fall of Jerusalem

14 "But when you see the abomination of desolation standing where he ought not to be (let the reader understand), then let those who are in Judea flee to the mountains. **15** Let the one who is on the housetop not go down, nor enter his house, to take anything out, **16** and let the one who is in the field not turn back to take his cloak. **17** And alas for women who are pregnant and for those who are nursing infants in those days! **18** Pray that it may not happen in winter. **19** For in those days there will be such tribulation as has not been from the beginning of the creation that God created until now, and never will be.

A Road-Map to the End (B)

20 "And if the Lord had not cut short the days, no human being would be saved. But for the sake of the elect, whom he chose, he shortened the days. **21** And then if anyone says to you, 'Look, here is the Christ!' or 'Look, there he is!' do not believe it. **22** For false christs and false prophets will arise and perform signs and wonders, to lead astray, if possible, the elect. **23** But be on guard; I have told you all things beforehand.

LUKE
The Fall of Jerusalem

20 *"But when you see Jerusalem surrounded by armies, then know that its desolation has come near.* **21** *Then let those who are in Judea flee to the mountains, and let those who are inside the city depart, and let not those who are out in the country enter it,* **22** *for these are days of vengeance, to fulfill all that is written.* **23** *Alas for women who are pregnant and for those who are nursing infants in those days! For there will be great distress upon the earth and wrath against this people.* **24** *They will fall by the edge of the sword and be led captive among all nations, and Jerusalem will be trampled underfoot by the Gentiles, until the times of the Gentiles are fulfilled.*

MATTHEW
The Coming of the Son of Man

29 "Immediately after the tribulation of those days the sun will be darkened, and the moon will not give its light, and the stars will fall from heaven, and the powers of the heavens will be shaken. **30** Then will appear in heaven the sign of the Son of Man, and then all the tribes of the earth will mourn, and they will see the Son of Man coming on the clouds of heaven with power and great glory. **31** And he will send out his angels with a loud trumpet call, and they will gather his elect from the four winds, from one end of heaven to the other.

Reading the Signs of the Times[8]

32 "From the fig tree learn its lesson: as soon as its branch becomes tender and puts out its leaves, you know that summer is near. **33** So also, when you see all these things, you know that he is near, at the very gates. **34** Truly, I say to you, this generation will not pass away until all these things take place. **35** Heaven and earth will pass away, but my words will not pass away.

MARK
The Coming of the Son of Man

24 "But in those days, after that tribulation, the sun will be darkened, and the moon will not give its light, **25** and the stars will be falling from heaven, and the powers in the heavens will be shaken. **26** And then they will see the Son of Man coming in clouds with great power and glory. **27** And then he will send out the angels and gather his elect from the four winds, from the ends of the earth to the ends of heaven.

Reading the Signs of the Times[9]

28 "From the fig tree learn its lesson: as soon as its branch becomes tender and puts out its leaves, you know that summer is near. **29** So also, when you see these things taking place, you know that he is near, at the very gates. **30** Truly, I say to you, this generation will not pass away until all these things take place. **31** Heaven and earth will pass away, but my words will not pass away.

LUKE
The Coming of the Son of Man

25 *"And there will be signs in sun and moon and stars, and on the earth distress of nations in perplexity because of the roaring of the sea and the waves,* **26** *people fainting with fear and with foreboding of what is coming on the world. For the powers of the heavens will be shaken.* **27** *And then they will see the Son of Man coming in a cloud with power and great glory.* **28** *Now when these things begin to take place, straighten up and raise your heads, because your redemption is drawing near."*

Reading the Signs of the Times [10]

29 And he told them a parable: "Look at the fig tree, and all the trees. **30** As soon as they come out in leaf, you see for yourselves and know that the summer is already near. **31** So also, when you see these things taking place, you know that the kingdom of God is near. **32** Truly, I say to you, this generation will not pass away until all has taken place. **33** Heaven and earth will pass away, but my words will not pass away.

MATTHEW
Being Prepared for the End[II]

36 "But concerning that day and hour no one knows, not even the angels of heaven, nor the Son, but the Father only. **37** For as were the days of Noah, so will be the coming of the Son of Man. **38** For as in those days before the flood they were eating and drinking, marrying and giving in marriage, until the day when Noah entered the ark, **39** and they were unaware until the flood came and swept them all away, so will be the coming of the Son of Man. **40** Then two men will be in the field; one will be taken and one left. **41** Two women will be grinding at the mill; one will be taken and one left. **42** Therefore, stay awake, for you do not know on what day your Lord is coming.

43 "But know this, that if the master of the house had known in what part of the night the thief was coming, he would have stayed awake and would not have let his house be broken into. **44** Therefore you also must be ready, for the Son of Man is coming at an hour you do not expect.

45 "Who then is the faithful and wise servant, whom his master has set over his household, to give them their food at the proper time? **46** Blessed is that servant whom his master will find so doing when he comes. **47** Truly, I say to you, he will set him over all his possessions. **48** But if that wicked servant says to himself, 'My master is delayed,' **49** and begins to beat his fellow servants and eats and drinks with drunkards, **50** the master of that servant will come on a day when he does not expect him and at an hour he does not know **51** and will cut him in pieces and put him with the hypocrites. In that place there will be weeping and gnashing of teeth. "

MARK
Being Prepared for the End

32 "But concerning that day or that hour, no one knows, not even the angels in heaven, nor the Son, but only the Father.

33 Be on guard, keep awake. For you do not know when the time will come.

34 "It is like a man going on a journey, when he leaves home and puts his servants in charge, each with his work, and commands the doorkeeper to stay awake. **35** Therefore stay awake—for you do not know when the master of the house will come, in the evening, or at midnight, or when the cock crows, or in the morning— **36** lest he come suddenly and find you asleep. **37** And what I say to you I say to all: Stay awake."

LUKE

Being Prepared for the End

34 *"But watch yourselves lest your hearts be weighed down with dissipation and drunkenness and cares of this life, and that day come upon you suddenly like a trap.* **35** *For it will come upon all who dwell on the face of the whole earth.* **36** *But stay awake at all times, praying that you may have strength to escape all these things that are going to take place, and to stand before the Son of Man."*

37 *And every day he was teaching in the temple, but at night he went out and lodged on the mount called Olivet.* **38** *And early in the morning all the people came to him in the temple to hear him.*

CHAPTER 11: THE COMING KINGDOM

MATTHEW
The Parable of the Ten Virgins

25 "Then the kingdom of heaven will be like ten virgins who took their lamps and went to meet the bridegroom. **2** Five of them were foolish, and five were wise. **3** For when the foolish took their lamps, they took no oil with them, **4** but the wise took flasks of oil with their lamps. **5** As the bridegroom was delayed, they all became drowsy and slept. **6** But at midnight there was a cry, 'Here is the bridegroom! Come out to meet him.' **7** Then all those virgins rose and trimmed their lamps. **8** And the foolish said to the wise, 'Give us some of your oil, for our lamps are going out.' **9** But the wise answered, saying, 'Since there will not be enough for us and for you, go rather to the dealers and buy for yourselves.' **10** And while they were going to buy, the bridegroom came, and those who were ready went in with him to the marriage feast, and the door was shut. **11** Afterward the other virgins came also, saying, 'Lord, lord, open to us.' **12** But he answered, 'Truly, I say to you, I do not know you.' **13** Watch therefore, for you know neither the day nor the hour.

The Parable of the Talents

14 "For it will be like a man going on a journey, who called his servants and entrusted to them his property. **15** To one he gave five talents, to another two, to another one, to each according to his ability. Then he went away. **16** He who had received the five talents went at once and traded with them, and he made five talents more. **17** So also he who had the two talents made two talents more. **18** But he who had received the one talent went and dug in the ground and hid his master's money. **19** Now after a long time the master of those servants came and settled accounts with them. **20** And he who had received the five talents came forward, bringing five talents more, saying, 'Master, you delivered to me five talents; here, I have made five talents more.' **21** His master said to him, 'Well done, good and faithful servant. You have been faithful over a little; I will set you over much. Enter into the joy of your master.' **22** And he also who had the two talents came forward, saying, 'Master, you delivered to me two talents; here, I have made two talents more.' **23** His master said to him, 'Well done, good and faithful servant. You have been faithful over a little; I will set you over much. Enter into the joy of your master.'

24 He also who had received the one talent came forward, saying, 'Master, I knew you to be a hard man, reaping where you did not sow, and gathering where you scattered no seed, **25** so I was afraid, and I went and hid your talent in the ground. Here, you have what is yours.' **26** But his master answered him, 'You wicked and slothful servant! You knew that I reap where I have not sown and gather where I scattered no seed? **27** Then you ought to have invested my money with the bankers, and at my coming I should have received what was my own with interest. **28** So take the talent from him and give it to him who has the ten talents. **29** For to everyone who has will more be given, and he will have an abundance. But from the one who has not, even what he has will be taken away. **30** And cast the worthless servant into the outer darkness. In that place there will be weeping and gnashing of teeth.'

The Final Judgment

31 "When the Son of Man comes in his glory, and all the angels with him, then he will sit on his glorious throne. **32** Before him will be gathered all the nations, and he will separate people one from another as a shepherd separates the sheep from the goats. **33** And he will place the sheep on his right, but the goats on the left. **34** Then the King will say to those on his right, 'Come, you who are blessed by my Father, inherit the kingdom prepared for you from the foundation of the world. **35** For I was hungry and you gave me food, I was thirsty and you gave me drink, I was a stranger and you welcomed me, **36** I was naked and you clothed me, I was sick and you visited me, I was in prison and you came to me.' **37** Then the righteous will answer him, saying, 'Lord, when did we see you hungry and feed you, or thirsty and give you drink? **38** And when did we see you a stranger and welcome you, or naked and clothe you? **39** And when did we see you sick or in prison and visit you?' **40** And the King will answer them, 'Truly, I say to you, as you did it to one of the least of these my brothers, you did it to me.'

41 "Then he will say to those on his left, 'Depart from me, you cursed, into the eternal fire prepared for the devil and his angels. **42** For I was hungry and you gave me no food, I was thirsty and you gave me no drink, **43** I was a stranger and you did not welcome me, naked and you did not clothe me, sick and in prison and you did not visit me.' **44** Then they also will answer, saying, 'Lord, when did we see you hungry or thirsty or a stranger or naked or sick or in prison, and did not minister to you?' **45** Then he will answer them, saying, 'Truly, I say to you, as you did not do it to one of the least of these, you did not do it to me.' **46** And these will go away into eternal punishment, but the righteous into eternal life."

CHAPTER 12: THE SAVIOUR OF THE WORLD

JOHN
Some Greeks Seek Jesus

20 *Now among those who went up to worship at the feast were some Greeks.* 21 *So these came to Philip, who was from Bethsaida in Galilee, and asked him, "Sir, we wish to see Jesus."* 22 *Philip went and told Andrew; Andrew and Philip went and told Jesus.* 23 *And Jesus answered them, "The hour has come for the Son of Man to be glorified.* 24 *Truly, truly, I say to you, unless a grain of wheat falls into the earth and dies, it remains alone; but if it dies, it bears much fruit.* 25 *Whoever loves his life loses it, and whoever hates his life in this world will keep it for eternal life.* 26 *If anyone serves me, he must follow me; and where I am, there will my servant be also. If anyone serves me, the Father will honor him.*

The Son of Man Must Be Lifted Up

27 *"Now is my soul troubled. And what shall I say? 'Father, save me from this hour'? But for this purpose I have come to this hour.* 28 *Father, glorify your name." Then a voice came from heaven: "I have glorified it, and I will glorify it again."* 29 *The crowd that stood there and heard it said that it had thundered. Others said, "An angel has spoken to him."* 30 *Jesus answered, "This voice has come for your sake, not mine.* 31 *Now is the judgment of this world; now will the ruler of this world be cast out.* 32 *And I, when I am lifted up from the earth, will draw all people to myself."* 33 *He said this to show by what kind of death he was going to die.* 34 *So the crowd answered him, "We have heard from the Law that the Christ remains forever. How can you say that the Son of Man must be lifted up? Who is this Son of Man?"* 35 *So Jesus said to them, "The light is among you for a little while longer. Walk while you have the light, lest darkness overtake you. The one who walks in the darkness does not know where he is going.* 36 *While you have the light, believe in the light, that you may become sons of light."*

The Unbelief of the People

When Jesus had said these things, he departed and hid himself from them. **37** *Though he had done so many signs before them, they still did not believe in him,* **38** *so that the word spoken by the prophet Isaiah might be fulfilled:*

"Lord, who has believed what he heard from us,
and to whom has the arm of the Lord been revealed?"

39 *Therefore they could not believe. For again Isaiah said,*

40 *"He has blinded their eyes*
and hardened their heart,
lest they see with their eyes,
and understand with their heart,
and turn,
and I would heal them."

41 *Isaiah said these things because he saw his glory and spoke of him.* **42** *Nevertheless, many even of the authorities believed in him, but for fear of the Pharisees they did not confess it, so that they would not be put out of the synagogue;* **43** *for they loved the glory that comes from man more than the glory that comes from God.*

Jesus Came to Save the World

44 *And Jesus cried out and said, "Whoever believes in me, believes not in me but in him who sent me.* **45** *And whoever sees me sees him who sent me.* **46** *I have come into the world as light, so that whoever believes in me may not remain in darkness.* **47** *If anyone hears my words and does not keep them, I do not judge him; for I did not come to judge the world but to save the world.* **48** *The one who rejects me and does not receive my words has a judge; the word that I have spoken will judge him on the last day.* **49** *For I have not spoken on my own authority, but the Father who sent me has himself given me a commandment—what to say and what to speak.* **50** *And I know that his commandment is eternal life. What I say, therefore, I say as the Father has told me."*

NOTES

1 Heading altered from original ESV heading.

2 Heading altered from original ESV heading.

3 Heading altered from original ESV heading.

4 Paragraph division added to ESV text.

5 Paragraph division added to ESV text.

6 All headings on these pages have been altered from the original ESV headings.

7 All headings on these pages have been altered from the original ESV headings.

8 Heading altered from original ESV heading.

9 Heading altered from original ESV heading.

10 Heading altered from original ESV heading.

11 All headings on these pages have been altered from the original ESV headings.